THE CATHOLIC SPIRIT

IS VOLUME

88

OF THE

Twentieth Century Encyclopedia of Catholicism

UNDER SECTION

VIII

THE ORGANIZATION OF THE CHURCH

IT IS ALSO THE

19TH

VOLUME IN ORDER OF PUBLICATION

Edited by HENRI DANIEL-ROPS *of the Académie Française*

THE CATHOLIC SPIRIT

By ANDRÉ RÉTIF, S.J.

Translated from the French by DOM ALDHELM DEAN

HAWTHORN BOOKS · PUBLISHERS · *New York*

First Edition, June, 1959

NIHIL OBSTAT

Carolus Davis, S.T.L.

    Censor Deputatus

IMPRIMATUR

E. Morrogh Bernard

    Vicarius Generalis

Westmonasterii, die XXXI DECEMBRIS MCMLIX

CONTENTS

INTRODUCTION

> The catholicity of the Church is not some law of
> sociology pledged to the service of an idea. In the
> last resort, the mystery of the Church, like her
> catholicity and her unity, appears to be a mystery
> of love and fecundity, like the reflection in time
> and space of the mystery of the Blessed Trinity
> itself.
>
> J. DE MENASCE, O.P.

In the course of history, the word *catholic* has had a strangely
chequered career. From being used by Greek writers
(Aristotle, Zeno, Polybius . . .) to indicate that which is
universal and general, it has become the proper name of the
true Church. It is as though God willed that this word should
be formed just in time for the Church founded by his Son to
make it her own. From the adjective *catholic* has sprung the
noun *catholicity*, denoting both the Catholic countries in
general and the character of the Church bearing that name.
It is the second connotation that will concern us in this work.

The important character of the Church that it discloses
has never—to our knowledge—been made the subject of a
deep and thoroughgoing study. A few pamphlets and excellent articles or chapters of books on more general subjects
have treated of the question, but we are still waiting for the
work that will summarize all we know on the subject. We
make no pretension of undertaking such a work here, for
neither the purpose nor the space allowed in this series per-
mits of it. We have been obliged to reduce our notes to the
utmost, so as not to embarrass or discourage the reader who
is not a trained theologian. Among the many masters we
have followed, we must mention Fathers de Montcheuil, de
Lubac, the great pioneer in this matter, Congar, and Mgr

Journet. This book is no more than a faint echo of their ample knowledge and wide erudition.

Our ambition is to provide the educated Christian public with the outline of a modern treatise on the Catholicity of the Church. The treatise will aim at being more doctrinal than apologetic, insisting more on catholicity as an essential property of Christianity, than on its aspect as a distinctive note of the true Church. We shall aim at giving to catholicity, in these "latter days" of a completed world, its fullness of dimension, its cosmic dimension. In short, these few pages will seek to be a commentary of Claudel's words in his Introduction to Albert Franck-Duquesne's *Cosmos et Gloire*:

"The activity of the Catholic Church is not limited to the world of souls; she has planted, to use the words of Isaias, her tent pegs on the very frontiers of creation. No part of God's work is foreign to her. Nothing of all that contributes to God's glory and the salvation of his creation escapes from her knowledge and her rule. She is responsible for the whole universe, and it is her work to bring to the final Sabbath the work of the Six Days. . . ."

BRIEF HISTORY OF THE NOTION OF CATHOLICITY

Christian Antiquity

The epithet *catholic* comes from two Greek words meaning "generally", "universally", "all things considered". However, from the dawn of Christianity, the word was used to denote, not only the meaning *universal*, but that which was orthodox, belonging to the true Church as opposed to heretical or schismatic bodies. This second meaning is not entirely lost, but we shall be concerned with the idea of a Church that is universal, as opposed to individual, or rather individualistic churches.

The first example of this use of the word is found in the Letter of St Ignatius of Antioch to the people of Smyrna (about A.D. 112): "Where the bishop is, there let the community be, just as where is Jesus Christ, there is the Catholic Church."

As Christ is the centre of the universal Church, so must the bishop be the centre of each local church. Forty years later, an account of the martyrdom of St Polycarp is addressed "to all the parishes of the holy and Catholic Church, wherever they are to be found". But already it seems that elsewhere the same author makes use of the word catholic to contrast the true Church with heretical sects.

From then on, Christians are conscious of belonging to a community that is universal, and are filled with admiration for its universal diffusion. This is the Church for which St Polycarp prays before enduring the flames of martyrdom. This is the Church envisaged by the author of the "Doctrine of the Twelve Apostles" (the *Didache*): "As the bread here broken was scattered over the mountains and hills, and having been gathered up became one, so may thy Church be gathered into thy kingdom from the very ends of the earth. . . . Be mindful, Lord, of thy Church, deliver it from all harm and perfect it in thy love, gathering that holy thing from the four winds into the kingdom that thou hast prepared for it."

This is the Church that Abercius, Bishop of Hierapolis, claims to have met everywhere:

I am the disciple of a Good Shepherd who feeds his flocks of sheep over mountains and in valleys, and whose great eyes see all. . . . He it was who sent me to Rome to contemplate the sovereign lady, to see the queen clothed in gold, and shod with golden sandals. There did I see a people who bear a brilliant seal. I have also seen the plains and all the cities of Syria and Nisibia beyond the Euphrates. Everywhere I found my brethren . . . and the faith led me in each place. Everywhere she nourished me with the fish from the stream (Christ), a great fish and spotless, brought to land by a pure virgin. Without ceasing, she gives her friends to eat of it. She has a most excellent wine that she gives with bread.

The first Christian writers were struck by the sight of a Church wonderfully spread through all nations and maintaining none the less her unbreakable unity. It is this unity, catholic and universal, that they contrast with the individualism of Gnostics and other sects. St Irenaeus writes:

> Without doubt languages differ (in the Church) throughout the world; but the power of her tradition is one and identical. The Churches founded in the Germanic lands have not some other faith, some other tradition; nor have the Churches founded in Spain, nor among the Celts, nor in the east, nor in Egypt, nor Libya, nor in the centre of the world. But just as God's creature the sun is one and identical throughout the world, so does the preaching of the truth shine everywhere, enlightening all men who wish to come to knowledge of the truth.

But the Church is not catholic solely because of her geographic diffusion. So we find St Cyril of Jerusalem, in his eighteenth catechetical instruction, explaining that she possesses catholicity because she teaches all dogmas to all conditions of men and cures all sinners. But he begins by telling of the universal diffusion of Christianity: "The Church is called Catholic because she extends from one end of the world to the other."

St Augustine exclaims, when attacking the Donatists: "I know not who it is who limits charity to the land of Africa? You must let your charity reach to the world's end if you would love Christ; for the members of Christ are spread throughout the whole world."

In very early days, this Christian faith found expression in the formulation of the Creeds, which became traditional from the time of the Council of Constantinople (A.D. 381): *Et unam, sanctam, catholicam, et apostolicam Ecclesiam.*

The Middle Ages

The great scholastic doctors [Fr Congar writes] are astonishingly faithful in accepting and setting forth the two aspects of

the idea of catholicity. Without neglecting certain aspects of
less importance, they show how catholicity develops in the
Church both by her diffusion that is truly universal (all times,
all peoples, all conditions of life), and also by the universality
of the truth set forth in her doctrine. He quotes St Albert the
Great and also St Thomas commenting on the Apostles' Creed
in a sermon preached at Naples: The Church is Catholic, that
is to say universal. Primarily through her local or geographical
catholicity, which spring from her diffusion throughout the
whole world . . . then from her catholicity in embracing all
conditions of men, from which none are excluded . . . finally,
she is universal in time . . . existing from Abel until the end
of time, after which she will continue in heaven. . . .

In another place he enlarges upon this notion of catholicity,
telling us that the Christian religion is Catholic because it is
accepted by men of all conditions, and secondly by reason of
the universal satisfaction that it affords to human needs, embracing them all in the fullness of life, and guiding them
towards happiness, not only spiritual but also bodily or
earthly. We cannot fail to notice the fullness, the modern
tone of such a conception.

In those days, Christians of the West, from the humblest
to the most cultivated, lived a life that was wholly within a
Catholic environment. Nobody questioned either the divinity,
the purpose or the catholicity of the Church. Everybody be-
lieved in her universal diffusion. The more learned among
them had long reflected on her ability to bring all men to
salvation. The supernatural realism of those days gave to the
notion of Christian universality both greater richness and less
scientific precision. From this springs an apologetic that is
more vital, more all-embracing. It was only later that the Protestant and pagan secessions of the Renaissance period
obliged thinkers to base their arguments for the catholicity of
the Church on new foundations, with the danger of inflexi-
bility and impoverishment. To appreciate the position of St
Thomas and his contemporaries, we must put ourselves in

the context of their time. Catholicity was their very life, and they felt no pressing need to prove its existence or to analyse its wealth of doctrine.

An article by Fr Labrunie describes in greater detail St Thomas's teaching on catholicity. The philosophical presupposition and the human principle on which it is founded is the universalism of the intelligence; a power that is a property of being, and so of the divine. By his universal royalty, Christ rules the whole of humanity; by his universal priesthood, he leads that humanity to God, the end of every creature. It is the Church's lot to spread throughout the world the fruits of the Incarnation, in every generation since Christ walked on earth. The Church is a continuation of the Incarnation. This universalism is thus found at the level of the intelligence, of God, of Christ and of the Church. We see then with what clarity and what magnificence the idea of catholicity is found within the mind of the angelic Doctor. With St Thomas, this notion "is the adequate meeting of his intellectual power and his theology of the Mystical Body of Christ".

Predominance of the apologetic aspect

Prior to the sixteenth century, only a few writers (such as James of Viterbo and Juan de Torquemada) had ever produced a systematic treatise on the Church, with arguments on its distinctive *notes*. Until then, theologians preferred to discuss the Church's *properties* and her essential characteristics, resulting from her being as such. The Council of Constantinople indeed spoke of the Church as one, holy, catholic and apostolic, but it is by no means certain that these characteristics were enumerated for the purpose of refuting heretics. Perhaps the intention was only to describe the true Church by her most obvious features. At all events, in the Middle Ages the doctrine was accepted by everybody in all serenity, and apologetic intention is all but absent in any writings on the subject. With the end of the fifteenth century came a great change.

Discoveries of new lands revealed the existence of numerous peoples who had no knowledge of Christian influence and accentuated the problem of the positive universalism of the Church. The severe pruning she suffered through Protestant secessions, added to the earlier mutilations caused by the Eastern schisms, reduce still further the proportion of Catholics in a henceforth better-known world. Then came the controversies with Protestants concerning the distinctive features of the Church of Christ. Later still, the influence of science on theology emphasized the importance of a quantitative notion of catholicity.

Canon Thils devoted his doctorate thesis to the profound and well-nigh exhaustive study of the concepts of the notes of the Church from the time of the Reformation down to the beginning of the present century. He shows clearly what have been the various attempts to define what it is that makes the Church's catholicity, the uncertainties, the regrets, the various currents that mingle, cancel each other out, or oppose one another. It is not for us to repeat the whole story here in detail, but only to recall its general trend. Of the four groups into which writers fall, according to the origin of their doctrine (Holy Scripture, St Augustine, St Vincent of Lérins and the Apostles' Creed), it is finally the last that predominates and casts into a theological tradition the scheme of the four notes: unity, holiness, apostolicity, catholicity.

As regards the last, theologians seem to feel a certain embarrassment arising from the difficulty of demonstrating the effective and visible universality of the Church. Bellarmine, among others, contents himself with the idea of a successive universality. According to this, the true Church is catholic provided that, while remaining the same Church, she is founded successively, in the course of the ages, in all parts of the world. This over-simplified notion was still being taught in theology in the last century. But all agree in emphasizing the spatial and geographical universality, without denying the existence of a catholicity that is more interior and of wider scope.

Nevertheless, objections made to this line of argument have obliged theologians to try and find a way of escape and to retire to stronger positions. At the beginning of the seventeenth century, it was held that the diffusion of the Church, although not complete, is nevertheless superior to that of any other Christian confession, and tends progressively to attain absolute universality. Later in the same century, this gave way to the idea of a moral universality joined to a catholicity of faith and time. But in the century that followed, the spatial notion is in the ascendancy, coupled with the universality of persons and upheld by the bond of unity. Finally, in the last century we see the beginnings of an idea of qualitative catholicity, since it has been impossible to give a fully satisfactory answer to the objections concerning both the number of Catholics and the countries reached by the preaching of the faith. Moreover, by this time a further difficulty had arisen— the extent of Protestant missions and the results obtained by them. Spatial catholicity was no longer the privilege of the Catholic Church alone.

Return to theology

This is generally considered to have been brought about by Father de Poulpiquet. His work has sometimes been treated as though it were the absolute beginning of all work on the subject. But in fact not only did Poulpiquet return to the great Scriptural, patristic and scholastic tradition, but also —as G. Thils has shown—he had more than one forerunner in earlier centuries. For example, Suarez insists on catholicity on principle, F. Hettinger in the nineteenth century on the transcendence of the Church as regards all individualistic bodies, Gutberlet on the Church's supranational character, and in 1903 Abbé Cloud wrote: "Jesus Christ willed that religion should be addressed simply to mankind . . . from this springs its wonderful power of adaptation to all races and civilizations. . . . The Church is Catholic through the appeal of her teaching, her practices, her worship, reaching to the conscience of all men, whoever they may be; she is Catholic by the satisfaction she gives to world-wide religious sentiment . . . Catholic by her spirit of holy conquest and missionary ardour."

Nevertheless, the merit of the young Dominican theologian was great; his early death was a loss to theology. As G. Thils writes: "In 1909, de Poulpiquet, by leading modern tendencies to a stage of development that has not yet been surpassed (1937), finally broke with the tradition that had always sought the realization of Christ's promise of universality made to his Apostles in some quantitative universality, and instead proposed to theologians a new kind of catholicity that he called qualitative catholicity."

The argument is simple and allows of no answer. Quantitative catholicity (geographical extension and number of adherents) is necessary, but insufficient in itself. The distinguishing mark of the true Church cannot be simply a matter of numbers, for in this case the early Church, with its necessarily restricted membership, would have been lacking in it. Moreover, catholicity of this sort is the visible sign and efflorescence of some more hidden property, a spiritual universalism to which all individualism is repugnant and which, for this very reason, acquires visibility and historical verification. This qualitative catholicity is therefore both a property and a distinguishing mark or note: a property, because rooted in the very being of the Church; a note, because it distinguishes in an external and visible manner the true Church from all other confessions and religions. This notion allows of no criticism: it is independent of arithmetic and is equally valid for all stages of the Church's history, even the early Church of Jerusalem, and is not to be confused with unity. In his book of 1910, returning to the theme of an article he had written in January 1909, Poulpiquet set out this doctrine in four well arranged chapters: the necessity and insufficiency of quantitative catholicity, qualitative catholicity as a property, the same as a note, the same as a motive of credibility. He thus came back, across the centuries of polemic with their over-topical and too utilitarian outlook, to the true tradition of the Church, and particularly to the doctrine of St Thomas and the Fathers. He offered a doctrine that had the attraction of giving predominance to the theological aspect, rather than to apologetics, always inclined to be too brief and limited.

Since his untimely death, the science of the Church has made gigantic progress, simultaneously with renewed missionary effort, the rise of Catholic Action, and the growth of a laity conscious of its obligations and militant in spirit. No need here to trace the various stages; it will suffice to give the names of a few theologians who have been the promoters of this progress in the particular field of catholicity: Fr Sertillanges, who has given back to this subject its magnitude, both human and divine; Fr de Lubac, whose book *Catholicism* (1938) has exercised an influence of which only future historians will be able to tell the depth; Fr Congar, a specialist in contemporary ecclesiastical studies; and finally Fr de Montcheuil and Mgr Journet, who treat of Christian universalism in all its theological amplitude. All that is best in the pages that follow owes its existence to them.

From now on, the Church's catholicity appears to us above all as a catholicity of principle and of duty, of fitness and of mission. Its aspect as a property outweighs its aspect as a note. It reaches out to man with all its virtues, its riches, its complexity, it is the meeting together of the universal love of God manifested in Christ and the universal nature of man, total humanity.

After thus setting forth, much too briefly, the general lines of a story that has always been troubled and confused and tinted with more shades than we have been able to note, we can now call upon the written evidence of Scripture and of the earliest Christian tradition, to show progressively what is the catholicity of the Church: how it is both an essential element and yet something progressive, a gift and yet something that evolves; a historical fact revealed in history; reaching in our days the totality of the human race in all its dimensions. Finally we shall conclude by considering the Catholic state of mind, which is for us the only practical conclusion of such a doctrine, whose present interest is greater than ever.

CHAPTER I

CATHOLICITY IN

SCRIPTURE

Our faith is founded on the witness of God revealed in history. This history has been recorded in Holy Scripture and also in that living tradition which enlightens and explains Scripture. Our first care will therefore be to study Scripture to look for the foundations and manifestations of catholicity. These pages, which are not intended for experts, will give no more than an outline of the question. Instead of accumulating texts, we shall only quote a certain number, as significant specimens that show the principal lines of development. The general appearance of scriptural universalism will nevertheless become sufficiently clear to act as foundations for the doctrine of later chapters, and will encourage those who have the taste and leisure to do so, to embark on deeper personal studies.

The two most normal divisions of this study would be the consideration first of the Old Testament then of the New, but we think it would be useful first of all to look at catholicity from the point of view of God and of Christ, and to show how its roots are in the Father's universal plan of salvation, and in the realization of the Incarnation and Redemption wrought by the Son. It is only from such a height that we can see and understand the universal mission of the Church, born of the Blessed Trinity and destined to bring back to the Father the whole of humanity.

CATHOLICITY FROM THE POINT OF VIEW OF GOD AND CHRIST

God's creative and saving plan

The Father's love extends to every creature that he has made, and especially to all men, of every race and every period in the world's history. His merciful design is revealed to us by St Paul in a passage that opens up boundless vistas of the heart of God. To Timothy he writes:

> This first of all, I ask; that petition, prayer, entreaty and thanksgiving should be offered for all mankind, especially for kings and others in high station, so that we can live a calm and tranquil life, as dutifully and decently as we may. Such prayer is our duty, it is what God, our Saviour, expects of us, since it is his will that all men should be saved, and be led to recognize the truth; there is only one God, and only one mediator between God and men, Jesus Christ, who is a man, like them, and gave himself as a ransom for them all (1 Timothy 2. 1–5).

The object of the prayer for which St Paul asks is twofold: it must be for all men in general and for rulers in particular. Yet the great majority of both one and the other group are pagans, and the Emperor was none other than Nero. . . . The intention of the prayer is to obtain for the Church a time of peace and tranquillity. Its motive is to please God who wills the salvation of all men. He wills this for two reasons: because he is God, the first beginning and last end of all; and secondly because his Son has died for all. The word *all* repeated four times by the Apostle shows clearly that this will of God extends to all men without exception. He does not will the salvation only of the Jews or only of Christians, nor even of just the elect. God's positive will is active and efficacious; from his side, he pours his grace out lavishly so that *all* men may be saved. Nothing but the free will of man can withstand God's loving design.

St Paul returns more than once to this affirmation of the universality of the Father's love: "Is God the God of the Jews only? Is he not the God of the Gentiles too? Of the Gentiles too, assuredly; there is only one God, who will justify the circumcised man if he learns to believe, and the Gentile because he believes" (Rom. 3. 29–30). And again: "There is no distinction made here between Jew and Gentile; all alike have one Lord, and he has enough and to spare for all those who call upon him. Every one who calls upon the name of the Lord will be saved" (Rom. 10. 12–13).

The love of Christ our Saviour is nothing else than the image and echo of the Father's love. Mindful of this, we shall understand better his own words: "The Son of Man has come to save that which was lost . . . it is not your heavenly Father's pleasure that one of these little ones should be lost" (Matt. 18. 11 and 14).

After having explained the plan of universal salvation to the Romans, St Paul gives free vent to his wonder and delight: "God has abandoned all men to their rebellion, only to include them all in his pardon. How deep is the mine of God's wisdom, of his knowledge; how inscrutable are his judgements, how undiscoverable his ways! Who has ever understood the Lord's thoughts, or been his counsellor? Who ever was the first to give, and so earned his favours? All things find in him their origin, their impulse, the centre of their being; to him be glory throughout all ages, Amen (Rom. 11. 32–6).

Christ the redeemer and centre of the world

At the very heart of the divine plan stands Christ who embodies and bears within himself all men of all time, and who has won for all the assurance and the possibility of salvation. Two passages from St Paul set forth Christ both as the principle of the conservation and the harmony of the world, and the principle of universal salvation (Ephesians 1, Colossians 1). The Father, the Apostle says, has blessed us in Christ with every spiritual blessing; he has marked us out beforehand to be his adopted children through Jesus Christ; he has made known to us the hidden purpose of his will, according to his loving design, centred in Christ, to give history its fulfilment by resuming everything in him, all that is in heaven, all that is on earth, summed up in him, revealing to us the immeasurable splendour of his power towards us the believers: "Measure it by that mighty exercise of power which he shewed when he raised up Christ from the dead, and bade him sit on his right hand above the heavens, high above all princedoms and powers and virtues and dominations, and every name that is known, not in this world only, but in the world to come. He has put everything under his dominion, and made him the head to which the whole Church is joined, so that the Church is his body, the completion of him who everywhere and in all things is complete" (Ephes. 1. 19–23).

Further on, the same letter to the Ephesians says that Christ, our peace, has achieved the unity of the world and unity among men.

It has been noticed how constantly recur those epithets that emphasize the human and cosmic totality that is summed up in Christ. The same idea is found at the beginning of the Epistle to the Colossians:

He is the true likeness of the God we cannot see; his is that first birth which precedes every act of creation. Yes, in him all created things took their being, heavenly and earthly, visible and invisible; what are thrones and dominions, what are princedoms and powers? They were all created through him and in him; he takes precedency of all, and in him all subsist. He too is that head whose body is the Church; it begins with him, since his was the first birth out of death; thus in every way the primacy was to become his. It was God's good pleasure to let all completeness dwell in him, and through him to win back all things, whether on earth or in heaven, into union with himself, making peace with them through his blood, shed on the cross (Col. 1. 15–20).

We can understand how St Paul, transported by this vision of catholicity, adds a little later: "Him (Christ), then, we proclaim, warning *every* human being and instructing *every* human being as wisely as we may, so as to exhibit *every* human being perfect in Christ Jesus" (Col. 1. 28).

Catholicity is here expressed in all its dimensions: every man, of whatever condition, is redeemed by and in Christ and must receive the proclamation of all truth. This holds for all times and all places, so that all mankind will form a single and universal body in the Church.

The return to the Father

The Church which came forth from God must return to God in its fullness by reason of its mission. Just as the sending forth of the Divine Word, fulfilled in the Incarnation of Christ, set in motion the missionary life of the Saviour among men, so the sending forth of the Holy Spirit, fulfilled in the Church, set in motion the missionary life of the Church in the fullness of time and its missionary enterprise among the nations. For the visible outpouring of the Holy Spirit must propagate itself and communicate itself in successive waves to all peoples of all times. The end and object of this plan, as the Greek Fathers recognized, is to bring back the whole of humanity through the Spirit to the Word, and from the Word to the Father. "Those who are baptized", says St Irenaeus, "receive the Spirit of God, who gives them to the Word, that is to the Son, and the Son takes them and offers them to the Father, and the Father gives them immortality."

In this way, thanks to the invisible missions of the divine Persons, creation which came forth from God is constantly returning to him.

In a few words, St Paul indicates this way of universal return to the Father and its consequences:

The head to which every man is united is Christ; so too, the head to which Christ is united is God (1 Cor. 11. 35). As all have died with Adam, so with Christ all will be brought to life. But each must rise in his own rank; Christ is the first-fruits, and after him follow those who belong to him, those who have put their trust in his return. Full completion comes after that, when he places his very kingship in the hands of God, his Father, having first dispossessed every other sort of rule, authority and power; his reign, as we know, must continue until he has put all his enemies under his feet, and the last of those enemies to be dispossessed is death. God has put all things in subjection under his feet; that is, all things have been made subject to him, except indeed that power which made them his subjects. And when that subjection is complete, then the Son himself will become subject to the power which made all things his subjects, so that God may be all in all (1 Cor. 15. 22–8).

In the Apocalypse, St John describes redeemed humanity: four and twenty elders sing a new song to the Lamb of God: "Thou, Lord, art worthy to take up the book and break the seals that are on it. Thou wast slain in sacrifice; out of every tribe, every language, every people, every nation thou hast ransomed us with thy blood and given us to God" (Apoc. 5. 9).

"And all creatures in heaven and on earth, and under the earth, and on the sea, and all that is in it" unite themselves to this act of praise.

Then the Seer contemplates the multitude of the elect, the brilliant manifestation of the catholicity of the Church in heaven: "And then I saw a great multitude, past all counting, taken from all nations and tribes and peoples and languages. These stood before the throne in the Lamb's presence, clothed in white robes, with palm-branches in their hands, and cried with a loud voice, To our God, who sits on the throne, and to the Lamb, all saving power belongs. . . . Amen, they cried, blessing and glory and wisdom and thanksgiving and honour and power and strength belong to our God through endless ages, Amen" (Apoc. 7. 9–12).

UNIVERSALISM IN THE OLD TESTAMENT

Two contrary trends

We see then that the vision of the Father and the Son is undeniably universal. How is this point of view to be revealed to men? Above all, how is God going to assure its triumph? Such is the question that we must now ask ourselves, and at least mark the principal stages and the main outline.

There is a temptation to be avoided here, one against which many authors have not been on their guard. With their eyes fixed on the final result, Christian universalism, they have projected the benefit and the scheme into the past. In their anxiety to draw from the Bible everything suggesting future catholicity, they have concluded too hastily and in too summary a manner that Holy Scripture is clearly and solely universalist. But this is to treat history cavalierly, to forget the necessary progress of Revelation and to suppress with one stroke of the pen a scriptural current that clearly flows in the direction of individualism and religious exclusivism.

There is nothing to be lost by admitting that the dawn is not full daylight, that the Bible contains, according to the standards of Christian judgement, both light and shade, and that, as regards the subject with which we are concerned, there are two tendencies there that alternately collide, mingle and oppose each other. With the help of God's grace, the conflict was resolved in the early years of Christianity, on the occasion of the famous "council" of Jerusalem, in A.D. 49. Until then the two currents jostle one another within the same plan, permitted by God as part of his general design, even though the selfishness and pride of men enabled a supercilious and disdainful individualism to triumph for a time. Three principal periods can be distinguished before the coming of Christ: a first stage, in which individualism predominates as a means of defence and preservation of a people; a second, when through the preaching of the prophets the conception of universal salvation gradually outweighs the opposing idea; and a third when, with the post-exilic Judaism, individualism is once again preponderant, at all events in Palestine.

Here we shall recount the history of the universalist view, since we are studying catholicity, but it is necessary first to summarize the principal elements on which the opposite attitude is founded and by which it is discerned. In the oldest texts of the Bible (e.g. the Canticle of Debora, Judges 5), Yahweh appears to us as the God of a clan or tribe, who leads his subjects to war and harmonizes as best he can the divers elements among the people during peace. This national God, who dwells chiefly in the mountains and the deserts, seeks to defend his people from pagan contamination, a wise attitude which will assure for Israel both its survival and the preservation of its faith. Several times indeed such religious originality was seriously threatened: at the time when the Israelites settled in Canaan (the time of Josue and the Judges) and found themselves in the midst of sedentary peoples who were more law abiding and civilized; at the time of the kings (Solomon), when pagan cults found their way into the palace through the influence of foreign wives; at the times of military defeat and sundry exiles; and finally in the latter days, when Hellenistic and Roman influence made itself gravely felt. At all these times and all through the centuries, Yahweh had to safeguard the faith of his people to prepare for the coming of the Messias.

Even in the period when a universalist conception of salvation was in the ascendancy, it was not without reserve or reticence. Many passages from the prophets show Yahweh crushing and exterminating the nations in the forthcoming days of the Messias (e.g. Ezechiel 25, 29), or at least reducing them to slavery and a position among the faithful of secondary rank (e.g. Isaias 49, 60 and 61). In spite of the real attractions of catholicity, the idea remained no more than relative; Judaism has never wholly freed itself from the concept of the nation and the race. The fact that it never reached true catholicity is what so clearly distinguishes it from Christianity, even primitive Christianity. It is true to say that in a certain sense Christianity is Judaism turned catholic and missionary.

Foundations of universalism

Genesis, at least in its final form, was not the first book written by the Jews under God's inspiration, but in the logical order it holds the first place and, with the books that follow it, gives us the foundations of that universalist conception of Judaism which, for a time, was to predominate with the prophets. The book of origins tells us indeed that Yahweh is the God of all men and all things, that all things were created, that all men have sinned in Adam and by themselves but that all have received in the person of Adam the promise of divine redemption. The rest of the book tells us the way in which God set about fulfilling his design. If he chose Abraham, it was not simply to save his family or his descendants, but so that all the families of the earth, all nations, should be blessed in him. So insistently does God emphasize his intention that no less than five times does he impress on Abraham that his vocation, his calling, has a universal extension.

Moses is almost exclusively turned towards the people whom he is to liberate, educate and form. As Pascal puts it in an enlightened phrase: "Moses for a people, Jesus Christ for all."

Nevertheless, the works that Moses accomplished and the divine interventions that so constantly recurred during the time of his government are filled, no doubt without his realizing it, with a signification that is universal. The miraculous deliverance of the Hebrews from Egypt is the sign of the Passover of Christ when the Son of God enables all men to pass from the dominion of sin to the kingdom of light. Every man is called to be plunged by baptism into the blood of

Christ, like the Hebrews in the Red Sea, and to cross over the baptismal Jordan that gives access to the Promised Land.

When that new Exodus, the return from the Exile, takes place, even pagans are not excluded from it. Ezechiel prophesies: "This . . . the Lord God pronounces. . . . At the end of forty years I will bring the Egyptians back from their countries of exile, restore them from their banishment, and in Phatures, the land of their birth, give them a home once more; there they shall be a kingdom of little account" (Ezechiel 29. 13–14). In the accounts of the early days of humanity and Israel, many elements are to be found that serve as a foundation for the universality of salvation: persons like Noe, Abraham and Moses; events like the coming out of Egypt, the crossing the desert, the occupation of Palestine. . . . On such a given basis of tradition, Jewish thought, inspired by the Spirit of God, was able to lay the foundations of an edifice in which all nations would, in time, have their place.

The universalist conception of salvation

It would be difficult to find in Israel, before the prophets, a clear appeal to the salvation of all mankind, a defined belief in the catholicity of religion and faith. Looking back, we can understand how David was the sign of the Messianic royalty, whose dominion was to embrace not only the chosen people but all the nations of the world. We know that Solomon's Temple was a figure of the universal Church, the dwelling place of the one true God. But the Hebrews of those days were too busy setting up and defending their kingdom to think about the evangelization or salvation of the pagans. However, the history of those times, written in later centuries, does include texts that contain a whisper of catholicity. For example, Solomon's prayer at the dedication of the first temple:

Lord God of Israel, thou reignest without rival in heaven and earth. . . . If the very heavens, and the heavens that are above the heavens, cannot contain thee, what welcome can it offer thee, this house which I have built? Yet, O Lord my God, do not let this prayer go unheeded, that sues for thy favour. . . . Is it some stranger, with no part in thy people Israel, who yet comes here from distant lands to do thy name reverence? For indeed there will be talk of thy renown, of the constraining force thy power displays, all the world over. When such a man comes to pray in this temple, thou, in heaven, in thy secure dwelling-place, wilt listen to the alien's prayer and wilt answer it. So all the world shall learn to fear thy name, no less than Israel itself; shall doubt no more that this temple I have built claims thy protection (3 Kings 8, *passim*).

But even these beautiful words, attributed to Solomon, retain their individualist and nationalistic flavour. The same chapter speaks of the children of the people "set apart, among all the peoples of the world, to be thy coveted possession" (verse 53).

And if God hears the prayers of his servant and of Israel his people, it is so that "the whole world may know that the Lord alone is God, there can be no other" (verse 60).

First of all, then, Israel came to realize that their God was the one God, and therefore the God of all. The next stage was a certain understanding of the merciful designs of Yahweh as regards other nations and all mankind. This new discovery was the work of the prophets. Here texts crowd one upon another, with ever growing clarity, showing an ever widening consideration of the pagan world. Amos shows Yahweh using one pagan nation to punish another (2. 1), and on several occasions he extols Yahweh's dominion over nature and the history of the world. Universal salvation gradually becomes bound up with the coming of the Messias. From the outset of his prophetic vocation, Isaias is possessed by the thought of the universal glory of God, and sees the Messias raised up as a sign of assembly for all nations: "There he stands, fresh root from Jesse's stem, signal beckoning to the peoples all around; the Gentiles will come to pay their homage, where he rests in glory" (Isaias 11. 10). Sion will then have a missionary part to play: "In the days that are still to come, the mountain where the Lord dwells will be lifted high above the mountain-tops, looking down over the hills, and all nations will flock there together. . . . The Lord's commands shall go out from Sion, his word from Jerusalem. . . ." (Isaias 2. 2–3).

The liberation of Moab and Edom and the conversion of Ethiopia are rumoured by the prophet: the peaceful reign of Yahweh is to spread over the whole world.

From then on the idea of universality is alive, and takes its place more or less rapidly in the general outlook. Jeremias is called to be "the prophet for the nations" and, by his conception of the New Covenant, frees religion from attachments that were too nationalistic. The movement slowed down with Ezechiel who urged the people to retire within themselves and to look forward to national restoration. Nevertheless, the prophet who foretold the rebuilding of the Temple suggests also the conversion of Egypt and even of Sodom (Ezech. 16. 53; 29. 13–14), and shows, in the vision described at the beginning of his book, God's empire over the whole world. The second part of Isaias has an even wider horizon: pagans will crowd towards the true God: "All the toil of Egypt, all the merchandise of Ethiopia, and all slaves from Sabaea shall come into thy power and be thine; they shall walk behind thee . . . crying out, God is with thee only; there is no God where thou art not" (Isaias 45. 14).

The third part of Isaias allows proselytes and eunuchs into the assembly for worship; perhaps even pagans will share in the priesthood. The same idea of universalism is found in Zacharias, Malachias, and in the little book of Jonas, written at about the same time, there is definite reaction against the tendency to isolation found in the other post-exilian prophets. Special mention must be made of the "Servant of Yahweh", teacher and redeemer of the whole world: "I have appointed thee to be the light of the Gentiles, in thee will I send out my salvation to the furthest corners of the earth" (Isaias 49. 6).

At about the same time, the idea of the Remnant and the Poor in Israel, whose prayer is based on the psalms, develops considerably. In the psalms there are constant appeals to all nations to praise God, to be converted and to enter into the true Kingdom. Mention must be made at least of the amazing Psalm 86 which binds all nations to Jerusalem, and Psalm 21 which Our Lord started to recite on the cross: "The furthest dwellers on earth will bethink themselves of the Lord, and come back to him; all the races of the heathen will worship before him; to the Lord royalty belongs, the whole world's homage is his due" (Ps. 21. 28–9).

An important step in the direction of catholicity was accomplished by the dispersion of the Jews as exiles in pagan lands —both those who were exiles against their will, as a result of the deportations following on defeats suffered by the chosen people, and also Jews who had emigrated voluntarily for commercial or family reasons. By the time of Our Lord, there were four or five times as many Jews among the dispersion than there were in the land of Israel. Such dispersions show in general a marked religious cohesion and a not infrequent inclination to make proselytes. As Tobias the elder said: "If God has dispersed you among heathen folk who know nothing of him, it was that you might tell them the story of his great deeds, convince them that he, and no other, is God all-powerful" (Tob. 13. 4).

By means of these proselytes, scattered through the Roman empire, Israel was preparing, without realizing it, for the diffusion of the Gospel and the catholicity of the future Church. But it was no more than a timid and imperfect preliminary sketch, like the first signs of dawn that announce the coming day.

The predominance of exclusivism

In spite of these attempts at diffusion, in spite of the appeals of the prophets to the idea of universality, in the last centuries before Christ Judaism closed its doors increasingly to any universalistic conception of salvation. Yet this was not what God willed for the chosen people. His ultimate wish was for Israel to be a missionary people, mediators between God and the world. But they on their side could see no further than their own restoration and national reconstruction. The influence of Esdras and Nehemias was all in this direction, as was also the abiding influence of Ezechiel. Jewish pride, wounded by Persian and Roman occupation, exalted by the heroic battles of the time of the Machabees, sought an escape and a compensation in a lofty and rude disdain for all pagan nations. When the Messias came, his message had no meaning for the religious leaders and doctors of the time.

Jewish theology scarcely retains the universalist emphasis of the divine promises made to the Patriarchs; it is only concerned with carnal lineage. On the other hand, God's cause is identified with that of Israel. God has separated them from all other peoples, and he hates the latter because of their sins; he considers them as of no worth, treats them harshly and refuses them the divine presence reserved for Israel. The Jews are therefore unsparing in their contempt. The Gentiles, they say, are not men; even the best of the *goyim* (foreigners) ought to be killed. They give them, and especially the Romans, the names of animals and the most despised animals at that. One single Israelite is worth all the Gentiles put together. Every day the pious Jew must thank God for not having made him a Gentile. This pride of race led to sentiments and attitudes of hatred, contempt and exclusiveness to which the resentful pagans replied by a fairly general antagonism to all Jews.

There is evidence of this pitiless and narrow mentality in the books then most treasured by the Jews: "As for idolaters and profane persons", says the Book of Jubilees, "there is no hope for them in the land of the living; and there will be no memory of them on earth; for they will go down into hell, into the place of their condemnation." And the Fourth

Book of Esdras: "I say all this before thee, Lord, because thou hast said that it was for our sakes that thou didst create the world; but as for the other nations, offspring also of Adam, thou hast said that they are as nothing, they are as spittle, and their multitude is like a drop of water poured into a vase." The Assumption of Moses sings of the reign of God: "Let him arise, God supreme, only eternal, and show himself so as to punish the nations and destroy all their idols." The famous rabbi Atriba, commenting on the Canticle "My beloved is white and ruddy", declares: "When they hear these songs of praise, the peoples of the world cry out to the Israelites: We wish to go with you, we want to look (for God) with you. But the Israelites reply: You have neither part nor lot with him; my beloved is mine and I am his."

The Pharisees and Scribes of our Lord's time are the representatives of this pitiless and exclusivist doctrine. The great lessons of the prophets are forgotten, catholicity has no meaning for them, in them exclusivism and national individuality have won the day.

UNIVERSALISM IN THE NEW TESTAMENT AND THE EARLY CHRISTIAN CHURCH

Christ's teaching

We have followed the evolution of the conflict between the two currents of opinion in the ages prior to our Lord's coming. In Christ, these two currents unite and the conflict finds its solution in his person and his work. There is, however, still one problem that needs to be solved: How are we to explain in certain words and attitudes of our Lord, the presence of elements that are clearly individualist and apparently contrary to catholicity?

First of all, what are these elements? Some of them are of no great significance or importance, such as the accounts of our Lord's childhood which were written, for the most part (the visit of the Magi and the Canticle of Simeon excepted), in an idiom that was strictly Jewish and nationalistic. This very fact is, moreover, a mark of their authenticity and fidelity of transmission. Neither can we successfully cite passages in which our Lord shows his attachment to the Jewish nation and the framework of Jewish mentality; texts such as Matthew 8. 12, where the Jews are spoken of as the sons of the kingdom; or again, Matthew 29. 28, where the kingdom is presented under the form of the Twelve Tribes of Israel: "You also shall sit there on twelve thrones, you who have followed me, and shall be judges over the twelve tribes of Israel." The universalism of Jesus does not indeed prevent his attributing to the faithful Jews a missionary task in the world and a special place in the Kingdom.

In actual fact, the only texts that raise any difficulty are those in which our Lord declares that his mission is to Israel and where he forbids the disciples, sent out on a missionary tour during his life, to visit pagans. To the plea of the woman of Canaan, he gives an answer that seems severe: "My errand is only to the lost sheep that are of the house of Israel. . . . It is not right to take the children's bread and throw it to the dogs" (Matt. 15. 24–6).

Even his words spoken on the occasion of Zacchaeus' conversion do not open up much wider horizons: "Today, salvation has been brought to this house; he too is a son of Abraham. That is what the Son of Man has come for, to search out and to save what was lost" (Luke 19. 9–10).

To his apostles he gives similar instructions: "Do not go, he said, into the walks of the Gentiles, or enter any city of Samaria; go rather to the lost sheep that belong to the house of Israel" (Matt. 10. 5).

Before giving the solution of the problem thus set, we must show that the doctrine and actions of our Lord are also strongly universalist. We have already noted that signs were not wanting in his childhood that presaged a universal mission. During his public life, much of his time was spent preaching in pagan territory, and even when in Jewish regions he was approached and sometimes besieged as much by pagans and Samaritans as by Jews. His doctrine always envisaged the salvation of the whole world, as can be seen in his parables, his many declarations where he speaks of pagans taking the place of unfaithful Jews and his repeated prophecies of world-wide evangelization. He prays for all men and for all those who will believe in him. Besides, as we see in the Beatitudes and the Sermon on the Mount, he never mentions the need of belonging to a particular race or nation as a condition of entry into the Kingdom. His teaching is for man as such, all men, of every age, of every nation. Christ brings to perfection the universalist lesson of the Old Testament.

At the same time he completely sets aside all idea of messianic nationalism, and refuses to let himself be proclaimed the Messias or temporal king; he is tireless in condemning the national pride of the Jews and foretells the abolition of their privileges. The struggle that he carries on against the Pharisees tends to liberate faith in the true God from the shackles of particularism. On the other hand, he gives a kindly welcome to the woman of Samaria and the Samaritan leper; he praises the faith of the Roman Centurion and after curing the possessed man of Gerasa he makes a missionary of him. In such a frankly universalist context, how are we to explain the attitude and words quoted previously?

We must distinguish in Christ a twofold mission, one personal and provisional, the other final and definitive which he will accomplish through the mediation of his Church. The world-wide field will only be opened by his death and resurrection. Before the Gospel was preached to the whole world, it was necessary for Christ to effect the redemption of mankind at Jerusalem which, according to the biblical conception, was the spiritual centre of the world. At Jerusalem, then, Christ had to preach, suffer, die and rise again. Such was the divine plan, witnessed to by messianic prophecy. A first phase, which we may call centripetal because centred in Jerusalem, was brought to an end through the mystery of Easter. Only then could the second phase begin, this time centrifugal, which would carry the Gospel to the ends of the earth. Until then the rights of the chosen nation would subsist, provided she did not put herself outside the picture through her refusal to believe. As B. Sundkler writes:

> The alternative particularism-universalism . . . has nothing to do with the biblical conception of the mission. . . . Nothing but a centripetal interpretation provided by a deeper comprehension of the centre of origin can give us a possible solution to the problem of *Jesus and the mission.* Just as Yahweh in the Old Testament entered into the Temple, so Jesus purifies the Temple and by doing so renews the world. For the Temple is the centre of the cosmos and the mission willed by Jesus is cosmic regeneration. We must always bear in mind the eschatological perspective in Jesus's idea of the mission.

Thus the supposed particularism of Christ is in fact at the service of a universalism that is truly efficacious and destined to become fact.

This is most manifest in the change of attitude seen in the risen Christ. At the Last Supper he had established the New Covenant in his blood, completing and replacing the Mosaic Covenant, still enclosed within the national framework. After the resurrection, he gives orders for a mission that is universal, and in words so emphatic, so coherent with all the doctrine of Christ and with the history of primitive Christianity, that rationalistic criticism, embarrassed by such words, has never succeeded in effectively questioning their validity. The final chapters of each of the three synoptic evangelists, the final chapters of St John and the beginning of the Acts of the Apostles demonstrate the inauguration of a universal Church, open to the whole world for all time, animated by the almighty presence of the Saviour. Read again, as an example, St Mark:

> And he said to them, Go out all over the world, and preach the gospel to the whole of creation; he who believes and is

baptized will be saved; he who refuses belief will be condemned. Where believers go, these signs shall go with them;
they will cast out devils in my name, they will speak in tongues
that are strange to them; they will take up serpents in their
hands, and drink poisonous draughts without harm; they will
lay their hands upon the sick and make them recover. And so
the Lord Jesus, when he had finished speaking to them, was
taken up into heaven, and is seated now at the right hand of
God; and they went out and preached everywhere, the Lord
aiding them, and attesting his word by the miracles that went
with them (Mark 16. 15–20).

Henceforward, Christ can exercise his proprietary rights,
his lordship over the entire world, and by his presence and
that of his Holy Spirit he will constantly assist his own faithful people.

Fr J. Bonsirven, in his *Les enseignements de Jésus-Christ,*
writes:

Christ will be equally visible by accomplishing the mission
received from his Father through the hands of his disciples.
A new era is about to begin. The disciples will become aware
of this as they perceive changes in themselves. . . . Above all,
their ministry is inaugurated in its definitive form: when they
were first called, they had been sent as missionaries to the
Jews for work that was temporary and restricted; now, their
appointed field of labour is the whole world, working as sub-
stitutes for their Master; yet the substitution is only apparent,
for it is always he who works through them. On several
occasions in the past, Christ had spoken to them and given
them instructions about this world-wide apostolate, which
would surely bring persecution with it; but it is only now that
they receive full, clear and explicit delegation. Their old outlook is completely upset; now at last they can grasp the
meaning of certain words and intentions of their Master; for
them and for us also they can only be understood in the light
of the resurrection and Pentecost, after and in baptism by the
Holy Spirit.

Christian expansion and St Paul

Thus the spirit of catholicity, after travelling its long road through the Old Testament, painfully and fighting all the way against a particularism that was sometimes triumphant, gained lasting citizenship through Christ and was able to begin its true mission. We shall not attempt to trace it all through the Church's history; we shall do no more than indicate the principal stages of its realization in primitive Christianity as recorded in the books of the New Testament.

Pentecost is the feast of universalism, of catholicity. The ideas of harvest, of jubilee, of the reply to Babel evoked by its agrarian origin, of the number *fifty* that gives the feast its name, as also the idea of universal reconciliation, all tend in the direction of catholicity. It is catholic through the diversity of those who listened to St Peter's discourse and the first converts to the Church, it is catholic again by the gift of tongues that foreshadows a Church in which all languages will be spoken and used for God's praises; it is catholic, in short, by the enlightenment and strength infused into the apostles with the gift of the Spirit of Jesus. The fruits of this outpouring of the Holy Ghost were only known clearly later, but it was on this day that God positively prepared the apostles for their universal mission.

During the first relatively calm years of the Church in Jerusalem, universalism progressed quietly. A larger place was given to the Hellenists (Acts 6), that is, Jews born outside Palestine, but living then in Jerusalem. Several deacons were chosen from among them and even a circumcised pagan, Nicholas, a proselyte of Antioch. Then came the death of Stephen, an important moment in the progress towards total universalism, thanks chiefly to the vigour and the novelty of his teaching. Without suggesting that there were violently opposed parties in the Church of that day, or that Stephen was by nature an agitator, we may admit with Fr Lebreton that "the Holy Spirit made use of Stephen to lead the Christian Church towards a greater independence as regards Judaism and its rites and laws".

The conversion of Paul, a Hellenist of Jerusalem, came soon after the martyrdom of St Stephen. Overthrown and mastered by Christ on the road to Damascus, he received from him orders to go and preach the new Gospel everywhere: "I will be thy deliverer from the hands of thy people, and of the Gentiles, to whom I am now sending thee. Thou shalt open their eyes, and turn them from darkness to light, from the power of Satan to God, so that they may receive, through faith in me, remission of their sins and an inheritance among the saints" (Acts 26. 17–18).

For his part, Philip baptized the eunuch, minister of the queen of the Ethiopians, and then preached the Gospel in Samaria and Saron. Peter and John came to visit these places, and it was then that Peter was constrained by the Holy Spirit to receive the first pagan into the Church, the centurion Cornelius of Caesarea. Until then, only proselytes of pagan origin had been admitted to baptism. However, the Church was spreading outside Judaea, and was particularly strong at Antioch, where the faithful were first called Christians, the name by which they were henceforth known. Those who had been converted on the day of Pentecost must have sown the seeds of the new faith, and other disciples, like Paul and Barnabas, proclaimed the need of belief in the Saviour Christ.

All these conversions were bound to trouble the minds of Judaizers and Jewish Christians who held that the only way of becoming a Christian was by becoming a Jew first and accepting circumcision and the Law of Moses. Were these rites still to be imposed on pagans, or could they be admitted straight into the Church which, although sprung from Judaism, was henceforth to be independent? The question was a grave one, and the step to be taken in progress towards catholicity was of capital importance. It is hardly an exaggeration to say that, in the whole course of her history, the

Church never had to face a more serious crisis. If, supposing the impossible, Christian universalism had not won the victory on that occasion, the Church would have remained a Jewish sect, with no pretensions of achieving universal expansion.

The problem was solved at the famous meeting in Jerusalem, sometimes incorrectly called a council. Peter spoke with authority:

> Brethren, you know well enough how from early days it has been God's choice that the Gentiles should hear the message of the gospel from my lips, and so learn to believe. God, who can read men's hearts, has assured them of his favour by giving the Holy Spirit to them as to us. He would not make any difference between us and them; he had removed all the uncleanness from their hearts when he gave them faith. How is it, then, that you would now call God in question, by putting a yoke on the necks of the disciples, such as we and our fathers have been too weak to bear? It is by the grace of our Lord Jesus Christ that we hope to be saved, and they no less (Acts 15. 7–11).

Barnabas and Paul then proceeded to tell of the miracles and prodigies that God had recently worked through them among the pagans, and James rose to recommend that the pagans who were converted to God should not be troubled with these other matters.

The final decision was sent in a letter, by the hands of Paul and Barnabas and a few companions, to "the Gentile brethren in Antioch, Syria and Cilicia":

> We hear that some of our number who visited you have disquieted you by what they said, unsettling your consciences, although we had given them no such commission; and therefore, meeting together with common purpose of heart, we have resolved to send you chosen messengers, in company with our well-beloved Barnabas and Paul, men who have staked their lives for the name of our Lord Jesus Christ. We have given this commission to Judas and Silas, who will confirm the message by word of mouth. It is the Holy Spirit's

pleasure and ours that no burden should be laid upon you beyond these, which cannot be avoided; you are to abstain from what is sacrificed to idols, from blood-meat and meat which has been strangled, and from fornication. If you keep away from such things, you will have done your part. Farewell (Acts 15. 24–9).

The way being now cleared, the principle of catholicity had been finally and officially acquired. The spiritual conquests that would follow were simply an application of this. Paul again set out on his travels round the Mediterranean and the roads of the Roman Empire. The spread of the Gospel was helped by the peace then reigning in that part of the world, by the existence of ways of communication and also by the independence that existed between various cities. It was possible to be expelled from one without receiving an unfriendly welcome in another, even when close at hand. Such a thing would be impossible with the centralization of modern countries.

Thanks to the intense and balanced zeal of St Paul, Christianity was planted and took root in Asia Minor, Macedonia and Greece; it also developed in Rome. It is likely enough that St Paul penetrated as far as Spain, in which case he would probably have visited Gaul on his way. He was not alone, however, in spreading the Gospel. His disciple Titus had gone into Dalmatia. Rome and southern Italy, the Illyrian coast and probably the coast of Provence and Spain all first heard the Gospel preached during the lifetime of the apostles. By then there were many flourishing Christian communities in Asia Minor, as we learn from the mention of them in the Apocalypse. At about the same time Carthage and Alexandria were reached by the new belief. Beyond the Roman Empire, Persia and perhaps the kingdom of Edessa and even far-off India were reached. Catholicity is already a reality seen in fact and the Church has within her sufficient power and dynamism to extend her beneficial influence to every continent and nation.

Such, in outline, is the primitive history of Christian catholicity. The idea is born in the centuries that precede the coming of Christ and makes considerable progress through the teaching of the prophets and the fact of the exile. Christ was born in a Palestinian world that was closed, inflexible, impervious to the idea of catholicity, so that his teaching fell foul of current opinions. The universalism that he preached cause scandal and indignation; reproaches in this connection were not wanting at his trial and condemnation. However, the risen Christ tore down every remaining veil, and sent out his disciples to the ends of the world. Little by little the Church realized the import of this unheard of mission and progressively freed herself from the Jewish bonds that still clung to her. In a short time, free and full of youthful vigour, in spite of the persistence among her faithful of a strong Judaeo-Christian element, she pressed on into new lands to win over pagan peoples and to integrate them into her already relatively universal community.

If one thing is abundantly clear as a result of this it is that catholicity in principle, the natural disposition to admit all men of all races, was an integral part of the Church's teaching from the very beginning and that the little Christian community was Catholic on the very day of Pentecost, even though it did not yet realize it. Catholicity of fact came about progressively with unsteady and discontinuous movement, sometimes advancing, sometimes falling back. We must now proceed to discover how it is that catholicity can be an essential characteristic of the Church and at the same time progressive.

CHAPTER II

CATHOLICITY: ESSENTIAL
AND PROGRESSIVE

We have seen in the first chapter how the idea of catholicity in the story of our salvation developed, took shape, and finally reached maturity with the coming of Christ. The account of its fortunes in the course of the history of the Church and in modern Christendom will be postponed until the last two chapters. We must now concern ourselves with consideration of the notion itself. In this way we shall recognize catholicity as an intrinsic property of the Church, possessed by her from the moment of her birth at Pentecost, and we shall see also how this property is realized more and more, becoming increasingly applicable as the years go on and new nations, languages and civilizations are integrated within the Church.

The Church is catholic in principle from the beginning; she has the ability, duty, power and vocation to admit within her bosom the totality of the human race. Little by little, as the centuries pass, mankind and all human concerns become increasingly imbued with and assimilated by Christianity. Catholicity is, then, an essential property of the Church and also a reality in process of formation; these are the ideas that will concern us in this chapter.

CATHOLICITY AS A PROPERTY OF THE CHURCH'S BEING

The twofold foundation

To begin with, we quote a few pages of Fr Congar, from the encyclopedia *Catholicisme* of J. Jacquemet:

Catholicity is that property of the Church by means of which the reality of what is multiple in her harmonizes with the reality that is one. It is the law in her which regulates the relationship between what is multiple and what is one. Thus it can be considered either from its multiple side or that of its unity.

Considered from the multiple point of view, catholicity is founded on the material cause of the Church, that is, human nature. For her substance she has all the wealth, the infinite variety of human nature, the infinite possibilities of the first Adam, expressed in many different ways. On one side, indeed, they represent a capacity for supernatural faith . . . and so an aptitude of supernatural faith to be a bond in which all men are united; on the other side, they show themselves in the infinite number of peoples, languages, cultures, situations or conditions, of spiritual experiences and ways of looking at realities. From this point of view, catholicity is that universality of all that makes up man in so far as he is capable of forming a united whole, of existing according to the conditions of that united whole, and of being brought finally to a transcendent unity.

Considered from the point of view of unity, catholicity is founded on the fullness of the grace of Christ who has been constituted by God chief of a new humanity and even a new universe. . . . Christ has been constituted by God the principle of a new existence of all things; this fullness of Christ includes his ability to save, cure, transform and bring back to God and the praise of his glory, the totality of all that is human in man, the totality of the powers of human nature and even the totality of the universe in so far as associated with man and destined for him. This catholicity of her Head is the principle of the Church's own catholicity. This catholicity of the Church is the universal ability of her principles of being and of unity, that is, the power she wields through the faith and the sacraments of faith by which she accomplishes the work of Christ throughout time and space, until we have all come to the perfection of the stature of Christ. Thus and then—but only then—will man truly be made in the image of God. The catholicity of the Church, in its essence, is that power possessed by its principles of unity (or being) to reach, transform, save, perfect and bring to unity the whole of humanity throughout the world, everything that receives or is capable of receiving some form of human vitality, the stamp and the movement of that creature, unique among all others, which, made in the image of God, has been made anew in the image of Christ. We see how this catholicity of Christ and of the Church, considered in all its dimensions, unites what one may call their "cosmism". . . .

We see also how catholicity, although it has two foundations, is one thing. It finds in human nature on one side and in the fullness of Christ on the other, the possibility of its existence, that is, its foundation. In itself, it is the character or property possessed by the Church to be at the same time rigorously one and limitlessly diverse; to be multiplicity in unity, proclaiming her unity, a unity rich with infinity of expression and realization. She sees that what is diverse and in parts exists according to the whole, and that the whole is one, with a unity not of poverty but of plenitude.

The fundamental passages just quoted are so dense and rich that it would be wise to read them through again and to comment on what they contain. The early Greek philosophers were obsessed by the problem of the one and the many. Here, this problem finds a superb and perfect solution. All that is human, all that man is or does, all that makes man what he is, finds its unity in Christ and in the Church. Making use of traditional philosophical expressions, we may say that human totality is the matter and the unity of Christ (or of the Church) is the form. There exists then a reality that is in the multiple order; it is made up of the wealth of human nature and the works of men. There is another reality in the order of unity, a divine reality that eternally contains in itself in God the Creator and Christ the Redeemer (the recapitulation and the centre of all humanity), the totality of what is human, and seeks to make coincide the principle and the fact, that is, the mysterious presence of humanity and of the cosmos in Christ and his presence made real in fact in the Church.

In the light of such teaching, we can understand the bold words of Fr Charles:

> The Church is much more than the means by which souls are saved; she is the divine form of the world, the unique meeting place in which the whole work of the Creator reverts to the Redeemer, and in which the Redeemer himself enters into possession of his universal heritage. She alone has the right to utter words that sanctify and pardon; to forgive sinners and sanctify all things. She alone, by filling up the gulf caused by original sin, transforms all things so that they become vessels and receptacles of the divine gift. But she is concerned not only with souls; it is her lot to maintain and consecrate the balance of the whole world and its value in eternity. She is not only the supreme teaching authority; she is the mother who embraces and the holiness that blesses. Doubtless, like life in the body, it is immortal souls who, among all created things, are on earth the particular patrimony of the Redeemer; but the universe is made up of more than the reunion of souls. The work of the divine Word is multiple without measure; from stars to insects, from volcanoes to swan's down, all is included in the divine splendour that it is for us, in and through the Church, to gather up and offer to God.
>
> To the question: Why the Church? the only answer is the further question: Why the kingdom of God? The Church is final; she will never be subordinated to some later creation. There also, all ends and all begins by an absolute and there is nothing more absolute than the order established by the Truth which is God (*Missiologie, 1939*, p. 85).

The Church, then, is the presence of God on earth, the extension of God's love which, in Christ, wills to renew all things, recapitulate all things, transfigure all things, save all things. It is a river of love that springs from the Blessed Trinity and returns to the Blessed Trinity, having meanwhile embraced, integrated, purified, deified all. Catholicity is as essential to the Church as it is to the Father, the Son and the Holy Ghost. The Father created all, the Son redeemed all, the Holy Spirit has sanctified all, and the concrete means of making actual this creation rendered conscious and grateful, this redemption, this sanctification, is the Church. And the means is also the end, for when God is all in all, then the end will come and the Son will render up his kingdom to the Father.

In the Church, the totality of Christ goes out to meet human totality in order to make a totality of a new kind, the heavenly Jerusalem in which are reunited all tribes and nations and tongues. According to the expression of Fr Sertillanges: "The Church is an organization of the infinite, if by the infinite we mean the divine Infinite and the creature by which it is reflected." And he adds:

> Evidently, then, if nothing is outside that, nothing is outside the influence of the Church in so far as she claims the allegiance of things and organizes them. God who created all things wills to bring all things to their due end, not for himself alone, but with us. And if the Catholic Church is the medium of his fellowship with us, then this Church is a power for total guidance and organization, although her uniquely spiritual outlook leaves abundant room for all other institutions without granting them licence incompatible with the unity of the last end and the exacting demands of that end (*Revue des Sciences Philosophiques et Théologiques, 1928*, pp. 721–2).

A few lines previous to the quotation just given, the same author wrote: "The Church is equal to the immensity of the universe, the immensity of time, the immensity of objects in life in every sphere, and the immensity of our hearts. How could anything bearing the name of man or of humanity escape from the net that she casts over the world?"

From whatever angle we look at it, catholicity is essential

to the Church; essential because the Church comes from the one universal God and it is her lot to bring all things back to him; because she was founded by the universal Redeemer and has the mission to bear his benefits everywhere; because she is enlivened by the universal Spirit who endlessly sings the glory of the Father; essential also because she has within her the ability, right, duty and power to gather all things within herself to offer them in homage to God and make of them the heavenly Jerusalem. To abandon her catholicity would be tantamount to abandoning her being; she is the living unity of the world, the unifying factor for all men. In her, the multiple and various achieve the complex harmony of a unity that is infinitely varied, infinitely rich.

Catholic since the day of Pentecost

If catholicity is an intrinsic property of the Church, it follows that the Church must have been catholic ever since her official birth on the day of Pentecost. A few words must be said about this first consequence of our proposition. We begin with a quotation from Fr de Lubac:

> Now a universal is a singular and is not to be confused with an aggregate. The Church is not Catholic because she is spread abroad over the whole of the earth and can reckon on a large number of members. She was already Catholic on the morning of Pentecost, when all her members could be contained in a small room, as she was when the Arian waves seemed on the point of swamping her; she would still be Catholic if tomorrow apostasy on a vast scale deprived her of almost all the faithful. For fundamentally Catholicity has nothing to do with geography or statistics. If it is true that it should be displayed over all the earth and be manifest to all, yet its nature is not material but spiritual. Like sanctity, Catholicity is primarily an intrinsic feature of the Church.[1]

God willed that the mystery of Pentecost should manifest, at the very outset, this catholicity in a manner that could be

[1] H. de Lubac, S.J., *Catholicism*, trans. by Lancelot C. Sheppard (London, Burns Oates, New York, Sheed and Ward), p. 17.

grasped by the senses, both through the miracle of the languages and through the presence of proselytes from all nations among Peter's audience. The Fathers of the Church took delight in bringing out the meaning of this mystery by comparing it with the account in Genesis of the dispersion of the people who tried to build the tower of Babel, and the account in Exodus of the promulgation of the Law on Sinai.

A few texts, chosen from many such, will serve to illustrate the universal significance of this mystery. In the Armenian liturgy we read:

> Spirit of goodness, thou hast enlightened by tongues of fire those who were assembled together in a common love. . . . The holy Apostles were filled with joy at thy coming; by speaking divers tongues they attracted men who would have been brought together by no other bond. . . . Thou hast used them to beautify the whole world, by holy baptism in the spirit, clothing them in new and resplendent robes . . . and thou hast, O living fire, been copiously poured out upon us; for the Apostles, once refreshed themselves, have refreshed the whole earth. . . . Today the churches of the nations are filled with joy and gladness that comes from thee, O lifegiving Chalice.

And in the Byzantine liturgy: "The people who presumptuously built the tower of Babel were formerly punished by the confusion of their language; today all languages are filled with wisdom by the glory of divine knowledge. . . ."

Adam of St Victor: "On the mountain the Law was given to the people, not in tongues of fire but on tablets of stone; in the Upper Room was given to a few men both newness of heart and unity of language. . . . The Loaves of Proposition offered as first fruits represent the two peoples received into one unique faith; the corner stone embraces the two, and of the two makes one people."

We find the same doctrine in St Irenaeus: "The Spirit", he says, "came down upon the Apostles at Pentecost, for it is he who has power over all nations to give them life and open up the New Testament to them; that is why, in the blending of all languages, they sang a hymn to God, the Holy Spirit bringing into unity widely different races and offering to the Father the first fruits of all nations" (*Adv. Haer.*, 3. 17, 2).

St Augustine is filled with wonder at the miracle of the tongues and its universal significance. He explains that this gift of tongues at that time was necessary "so as to show that all nations were to learn to believe in Christ. But once this fact had been accomplished there would be no further need of the miracle". He returns to the same theme later:

> The fact that the first disciples, on whom the Holy Spirit came down, spoke in the languages of all people is a symbol of this union (of the Church). It is by means of languages that different human societies establish union with each other. It was only right, therefore, that the society of the children of God and members of Jesus Christ that was to include all nations, should be foreshadowed by the gift of all languages. This gift of tongues was, then, a proof that they had received the Holy Spirit, and today the proof that a Christian has received the Holy Ghost is that he is united to the Church by the bond of peace that embraces all nations. . . . One man alone spoke all languages, because the Church was to unite all languages in her own unity (*Enarr.* in Ps. 130; *Serm.* 70. 17; *Serm.* 175. 3).

We see, therefore, that the mystery of Pentecost is the feast of Christian universalism. From then on the Church has a power and a vocation that are universal. The first Christian writers were well aware of this. In the introduction we noted that the epithet *Catholic* was used by St Ignatius of Antioch at the beginning of the second century. From then on this use of the word became traditional, so that Pacianus would later write: "Christian is my name, Catholic my surname (*cognomen*)."

Even more striking is the unrestricted use of the word *catholica* as a noun designating the Church, which seems to have been customary from the beginning of the third century and was in current use until nearly the seventh. It is even found much later in the works of St Bernard. Thus from her very birth, no matter how small she was, the Church was conscious of her catholicity, that is to say her universality in principle and by right, of her power to include all men and all civilizations, of the impetus that drew her towards the most distant lands. And this, without any alteration of her being or the least detriment to her unity. This is clearly illustrated by the title of one of the works of St Cyprian, "Concerning the Unity of the Universal Church" (*De unitate Ecclesiae Catholicae*).

The Church is catholic from her very earliest days because she is the continuation of Christ. As Bossuet says, she is "Jesus Christ, diffused throughout the world and communicated to men". From the day of Pentecost she possesses all the principles of being and of unity which enable her to embrace, in her desire and her intentions, the whole world. In the same strain, Fr Congar says: "The catholicity of the Church is the universal capacity of her unity. She is the 'perfecting' of Christ, his expansion and his fulfilment in humanity; the entry of his salvation and as it were his mystical incarnation in every living human being. For each man personally and for the whole of humanity, she is the gathering together, the accomplishment and the fullness in unity. She is our Peace in Christ" (*Chrétiens désunis*, p. 148).

The universal means of salvation

A further consequence of the principles set down at the beginning of this chapter is that the Church is the universal and sole means of salvation. If the Church, by reason of her very being, embraces the whole of humanity, if she is utterly one and is the divine form of the world, it follows that she is also the unique instrument for the world's salvation. This brings us to the immense question of man's salvation, the salvation of all men, a question that we can do no more than touch upon in a few pages. And the matter is so much more vast, distressing and mysterious since it must include not only the millions of pagans who lived before Christ and will live after him but also all the millions who lived prior to his coming.

At least we have one fixed tenet of our faith that will give light to our purpose. No man can be saved apart from Christ; no man has ever reached salvation without passing through Christ in some way or another. Moreover, we know that in fact men of all times have been redeemed by Christ; have been able, in a mysterious and hidden manner, to apply to themselves the fruits of that redemption, and by their personal correspondence with the grace merited by Christ have reached the state of the blessed and the final meeting with the living God. Now we also know that there is complete identity between Christ and the Church, so that the traditional saying "Outside the Church no salvation" means, in the last resort, "Outside Christ no salvation". For a believer this is obvious, and at once destroys, if not the mystery, at least anxiety on the question of man's salvation. There is not the least doubt, therefore, that from this point of view also the Church is Catholic and universal; she is the agent of universal salvation.

Nevertheless, we must try to be more explicit in the matter of the Church's part in the salvation of non-Christians, and at least to indicate certain pointers towards a solution. There is no want of passages from Scripture or pronouncements of the Church to act as signposts on the road we have to follow. God wills with an efficacious will (which nothing but the real freedom of man can thwart) the salvation of all men and that all should come to the knowledge of the truth. Universal salvation comes to humanity by the unique mediator between God and man, the man Christ Jesus, for Jesus died for the salvation of all, and there is no category of men excluded from his saving influence. There is no salvation possible outside the one visible Church of Christ, but at the same time the proposition holding that grace is not given to those apparently outside the visible Church is condemned. Pius IX declared that persons in good faith, who know nothing of the means of salvation through no fault of their own, can in fact be saved. We must conclude, then, that they are saved through some mysterious and invisible relationship with the visible Church of Christ. In recent times, the Church took a firm stand once again against the assertion of the American Jesuit Fr Feeney that those who are visibly outside the true Church cannot be saved.

At no time in history, then, have real means of salvation been wanting to mankind. In other words, the Church, like Christ, extends her saving influence over all men of all times, and in this sense, as the Fathers of the Church have frequently declared, she has always existed. St Leo the Great says, "The 'sacrament' of man's salvation has known no interruption at any time in the past. . . . In every age, by divers means and sundry ways, divine goodness has provided for the salvation of the human race, and with great kindliness has Providence poured out her countless gifts on all men in years gone by." What were the means used in this action of the universal Church? The first was for pagans who lived before Christ and also for those who have lived and still live since his coming: this was the religious mediation of creation, a supernatural mediation between the saving God who predisposes man and the genuine believer who responds to the divine advances through the promptings of grace. This mediation has an intrinsic relationship with Christ, the creator and judge. Like Christ, her head and her pattern, the Catholic Church recapitulates within herself the whole organization of salvation. Because of this universal fundamental principle, the Church has always been present and always will be present to every man born into this world. For the same reason, the Church was and is anonymously present to all men, and all men can really and from the beginning enter the Church without realizing it.

Over and above this fundamental mediation and in harmony with it, there are three kinds of institutional mediations: in the pagan world, they are the rites and elements of natural religion which are a simple material preparation for the Church; in the Jewish world, institutional Judaism is the formal preparation for institutional Christianity; finally, this latter is the recapitulation and final renewal of all that went before, so that Tertullian could cry out to God, "O Christ, ancient in what is new and new in what is ancient!" Every sound religious element that existed or exists in the humanity of all ages (certain rites and religious practices of pagans, of Islam, of the Mosaic law, and also such means of salvation as have been retained by dissident Christians), all belong to the one true Church of Christ, as to Christ himself, all is a form of the active and life-giving presence of the Church, and, for her, is a means of sanctification and salvation. She does not seek to destroy what is healthy but to bring it to fulfilment and perfection. It is not for her to disown her hidden, inchoate and unnamed presences, but to help them to achieve their end and become palpable manifestations of reality and truth.

Such a perspective should take us back to those passages in which Christian writers have extolled the Church's presence at all times and in all ages and acclaim this pre-history of hers wherein is already to be found the beginning of her saving and beneficent mission.

"Our Saviour", writes Paschasius Radbertus, "has a vine, the universal Church, which is gathered together from the just Abel until the last of the elect to be alive at the end of the world. . . . And so, all those who have been saved from the beginning of the world are in the Church like branches attached to the parent stem. . . . All form a single Church and a single vine which propagates itself through its union with the parent stem that is Christ."

And Newman:

> What man is amid the brute creation, such is the Church among the schools of the world; and as Adam gave names to

the animals about him, so has the Church from the first looked round upon the earth, noting and visiting the doctrines she found there. She began in Chaldea, and then sojourned among the Canaanites, and went down into Egypt, and thence passed into Arabia, till she rested in her own land. Next she encountered the merchants of Tyre, and the wisdom of the East country, and the luxury of Sheba. Then she was carried away to Babylon, and wandered to the schools of Greece. And wherever she went, in trouble or in triumph, still she was a living spirit, the mind and voice of the Most High; "sitting in the midst of the doctors, both hearing them and asking them questions"; claiming to herself what they said rightly, correcting their errors, supplying their defects, completing their beginnings, expanding their surmises, and thus gradually by means of them enlarging the range and refining the sense of her own teaching.[2]

These developments enable us to describe a new form of catholicity: universality in time. Just as Christ is essential to the harmony of the dialogue between every man and God, since no man goes to the Father except by the Son, so also, with Christ and in Christ, the Church is an essential part of this dialogue, for man can only reach Christ in and through the Church. It is certain that all communication with God and all salvation finally resolves itself into an act of one person on another, the reply to the divine invitation. But this act has of necessity its social aspect, it is necessarily related to the presence and the being of the Church, the mediatrix of truth and salvation. Every child of God, without exception, is a child of the Church. The fact that men do not realize this makes no difference to the fact any more than a savage isolated on a desert island ceases to be a member of the human family although he thinks himself to be unique in the world. All true charity has a social character, which accounts for the fact that every man healed by grace, aspires not only

[2] *Essays Critical and Historical*, XI: *Milman's View of Christianity* (1871, Vol. II, p. 232). Quoted by de Lubac, *op. cit.*, p. 271.

after his own individual salvation, but after a general salvation, to be sought for in communion with all men, and in visible communion with them.

Such is the universal motherhood of the Church which embraces the centuries of pre-history and history just as it does all continents and nations. In a certain sense one may apply to these men of all times and places the words of St Maximus to the baptized sons of the Church: "Men, women, children profoundly divided in nationality, race, language, walk of life, work, knowledge, rank or means . . . all these she recreates in the Spirit. On all in the same measure she imprints a divine character. All receive of her a single nature which cannot be divided and by reason of which their many and deep differences can no longer be held in account."[3]

It remains evident that the normal end of human destiny is eternal salvation by the Catholic faith, that man must search for light by every means in his power, that the Church must do the impossible to reveal that complete light to him. Both the glory of God and of Christ, the splendour of the Church and the good of souls demand it. If a man in good faith can come to salvation through some secret attachment to the visible Church, everything demands that he should come to this visible Church openly and fully. The germ of salvation that is in him must be protected and brought to fruition by adhesion to the true faith. The fact that the Church is the universal organ of salvation only reinforces and makes more urgent her missionary duty. As a body, Christians are responsible for the salvation of the world; to a certain extent its realization depends on them, and the Church will never cease to extend her borders, as Pius XII says in the Encyclical *Evangelii praecones*: "with a step that daily grows more rapid, until the furthest and most unknown dwelling is reached, the most distant and unknown man is reached".

[3] *Mystagogia*, c. 1 (P.G. 91. 665–8), slightly abridged translation, quoted by de Lubac, *op. cit.*, p. 19.

CATHOLICITY: A REALITY IN PROCESS OF FORMATION

These last lines show us that the catholicity of the Church is both a reality with which she is endowed and also a reality in process of formation. From the very first day the Church is essentially catholic and yet it is progressively that she unfolds this catholicity in the course of the ages and makes it live. Here we may turn to another passage of Fr Congar's which follows that quoted earlier. He has just alluded to the two foundations of catholicity (the fullness of Christ and the fullness of humanity) and goes on to show how this catholicity is at the same time a unity and a diversity.

In this connection we may say that catholicity is a property of the Church that is both actual and virtual. As the universal extent of the principles of the Church's unity, we may call it an actual gift, just as that unity is an actual gift, given ever since Pentecost, but at the same time it is possible for it to be brought into effect or made actual more completely. It is always an actual fact in the Church, because within the very principles of her being, the Church possesses this universal ability; and also because what is multiple within her is regulated according to the whole, and the whole is open to what is multiple. It is easy to see how much more deeply this goes than the level of mere quantity. Nevertheless, this catholicity is also still in process of actualization, in the sense that her principles of unity have not yet found the fullness of their applications and possible expressions, so that what is multiple within her has not yet had its last say. That is why the programme of catholicity is open to every apostolic or missionary possibility, and cannot be considered complete until the whole of the substance of the First Adam shall have passed into that of the Second; or again, as the prayer following the second prophecy at the Easter vigil says, "Grant that the whole world may join the ranks of Abraham's descendants and share the prerogatives of Israel" (*ut in Abrahae filios et in israeliticam dignitatem totius mundi transeat plenitudo*). The programme of catholicity, therefore, is essentially missionary or apostolic, and yet one that respects various cultures, forms of spirituality, nationality, languages and liturgies; in a word, all that diversity which consents to "accord with the whole" . . . and this is why we spoke of two foundations. Catholicity is not founded solely in the fullness of Christ, but virtually also in the fullness of all that he has received as his heritage (Ps. 2. 8; Heb. 1. 2). It receives its being not only from on high, from Christ, but also from below, from men and peoples in whom Christ "is complete". How the two foundations come to unity could be demonstrated by developing a theology of Christ as final cause and measure of creation, so that not without reason he bears that title by which he designated himself in a mysterious manner "the Son of Man".

The power that brings this programme to realization can be none other than the Holy Ghost in union with the apostolic body, the Spirit of Pentecost which is also the Spirit of Christ; he who, coming down on *each* of the apostles *assembled together* in the unity of love, brought it about that from that moment the Church should both speak all languages and have but one heart and one soul.

We shall try to elucidate these dense pages by certain developments which will show the necessity in principle and the existence in fact of the Church's catholicity that is both concrete and actual. The necessity of principle in this progress springs from the fact that if the Church, from its beginnings, possessed the power of integrating the universe, it is inevitable that she brings this to pass progressively with and in time. The first Christian community was too restricted to contain within itself men of all races and ages. It was a living body endowed with a universal dynamism but subject to that human "becoming" which little by little would spread throughout the world.

The parables of the Kingdom foretold this. It would grow like the harvest which produces first the blade then the ear and then the full corn in the ear; like the grain of mustard seed that grows into a great tree; like the leaven that causes the whole human dough to be leavened (Matt. 13, Mark 4, Luke 13). For his part, St Paul prefers the image of a body that grows and develops. He speaks of the building up of the body of Christ "until we all realize our common unity through faith in the Son of God, and fuller knowledge of him. So we shall reach perfect manhood, that maturity which is proportioned to the completed growth of Christ. . . . We are to follow the truth, in a spirit of charity, and so grow up, in everything, into a due proportion with Christ, who is our head. On him all the body depends; it is organized and unified by each contact with the source which supplies it; and thus, each limb receiving the active power it needs, it achieves its natural growth, building itself up through charity" (Ephes. 4. 13–16). The other metaphor used by the Apostle, that of the building, appeals to the same idea of progress and construction.

It is scarcely necessary to justify the existence in fact of progress in the growth of the Church. Starting on the day of Pentecost with a handful of Christians, she numbers more than 460 million souls at the present day; she has reached all races, all latitudes and morally the whole earth. The attempt has been made, though it can be no more than approximate, to give the respective number of Catholics in each past century. It is enough to illustrate the fact by the extraordinary diffusion of the faith in the first Christian centuries.

The Acts of the Apostles describe this initial expansion and growth of the Word; Loisy characterizes this Christian evangelization as "sort of communicative agitation, even a contagion . . . a world-wide epidemic . . . a contagion of hope". One of the earliest Christian historians, Eusebius of Caesarea, makes no secret of his wonder when faced with the overwhelming progress of the new faith.

It was thus, thanks no doubt to heavenly power and aid, that the doctrine of salvation, like the rays of the sun, suddenly lighted up the whole world. Immediately, following the

Holy Scriptures, the voice of the divine evangelists and apostles resounded throughout the world and their words to the extremities of the universe. And indeed, in every town and village, as in an overflowing threshing floor, Churches sprang up, thousands strong and filled with the faithful. Those who had been held in the ancient sickness of superstitious idolatry, following the old errors of their ancestral tradition, now, by the power of Christ shown in the teaching and the miracles of his disciples, were delivered from such cruel masters and freed from overbearing chains. Rejecting idolatrous polytheism, they acknowledged that there is but one God, the unique creator of all things, and they paid him honour by observing the laws of true piety, by a divine and rational worship which has been poured forth by our Saviour upon the human race (*Hist. Eccl.* 2. 3).

All through the centuries this forward movement of the Church goes on; she is constantly reaching new territories, new continents, and her missionary story is the proof of the continued progress of her catholicity of principle.

This doctrine and the quotations given include several lessons and consequences. The law of growth is deeply inscribed on the heart of the Church, but because of circumstances she has sometimes to endure darkness and a slowing down of her progress. Fr de Moncheuil, in his *Aspects de l'Église*, says:

The Church has within her the power to assimilate and transform the whole of humanity, even to its deepest fibres, and it is her duty and her wish to display this power to its fullest extent. It is not a growth that must continue, like that of the human body, until it reaches its full stature. Christians do not know in advance what will be the success of their efforts, either in extension or depth. It is possible for the Church to experience times of stagnation, even retreat, both in the number of her faithful children and in the fervour of the Christian nucleus. She has already experienced this. But on the other hand, she will never know a period of old age, when strength necessarily declines and the whole organism sinks irretrievably to death. The life that vivifies the Church renders her ever capable of new expansion without, and ceaseless renewal within. In this sense, the Church is always young, always able to grow. Never for her that fatal moment when she can do no more than keep going, awaiting her final decline. And whatever the vicissitudes through which she may have to pass, the will to spread without ceasing to the very limits of humanity remains ever in her.

So, although the catholicity of the Church seems sometimes to be in a decline by reason of schisms and calamities, when whole nations abandon her and pass out of her orbit, she nevertheless compensates for these losses by new gains and further growth elsewhere. Bossuet developed the idea of the torch of Christ borne throughout the world (*Œuvres Oratoires*, VI, pp. 80 and 119). No isolated or individual "church" has the promise of eternity. History shows us the ruin of sometime flourishing Christian communities in North Africa and the Near East owing to the onrush of Islam, and the amputations suffered in eastern and northern Europe at the time of the schism of the Eastern Orthodox and the Protestant revolution. Such disasters can happen again.

If the catholicity of the Church is never complete, never fully actualized, the important thing is that Christians should ever have at heart the full realization of that catholicity, and help it on in a practical manner by their prayers, their support of missionary endeavour and, if necessary, their very life. This point will be touched on again at the end of this work, but it depends upon us to see that the Church is ever deserving more and more of her title of Catholic, in a visible and tangible manner; she counts on our efforts, our prayers, our whole-hearted generosity.

CHAPTER III

CATHOLICITY IN HISTORY

Abbé Zundel, in one of his works, asks, "Is it really possible to write the *history of the Church*?" And he answers, "No, because the Church is something interior. To speak of the history of the Church is, for us, necessarily to speak of the exterior aspect of divine occurrences." In spite of this discouraging opinion, we intend to try in this chapter to see the history of the Church from the point of view of her catholicity. We shall look at the matter from three different angles: the Church's exclusion of all particularism, the special case of the Eastern Churches, the universal adaptation of Christianity. The first aspect shows the Church's wonderful aptitude to detach herself from all that could set limits to her or enslave her within the framework of what is merely human. The second brings out clearly the liturgical and cultural universality too little appreciated by Christians of the West. The third unfolds the wealth and diversity of the Church's attitude towards the inheritance of different ages and nations.

THE EXCLUSION OF ALL PARTICULARISM

In his book *L'Église Catholique*, Fr de Poulpiquet explains this aspect of catholicity in a passage that is worth quoting:

This spiritual universalism of catholicity is diametrically opposed to all forms of particularism that would reduce religion to the level of humanity and consequently thwart its propensity for diffusion. What are these forms? The three most striking would seem to be, first, the particularism of the

"I", or religious individualism. It consists of treating onself as the measure of all things and an inordinate regard for one's own opinion. The result of private interpretation applied to the religion of Jesus would be to subject all dogma to human reason and cause all mystery to disappear.

Secondly, there is that form of particularism that is political, philosophical, moral, economic, etc. . . . which some group or other is constantly extolling in the midst of some civilized and living nation. Its effect would be to fetter the lot of the Gospel to that of questions dealing solely with this world's problems.

Finally there is national particularism which, instead of rendering to Caesar what is Caesar's, and to God what is God's, makes use of the Gospel as an agent for its own internal and external domination. . . .

In the course of ages, the Roman Church has always been able to keep aloof from such forms of particularism which, with the dissident sects, have altered, humanized or materialized the universalism of the religion of Jesus and so, inevitably, have hindered the progress of its diffusion. It is by reason of her holiness that the Church has been able to maintain and defend her catholicity.

Instead of developing this theory we shall endeavour to provide its historical justification in no more than a mere outline which would require, for completeness, to be amply furnished with examples. Nevertheless, it will be enough if we can show how the Church, ever threatened in her universalism, sometimes implicated and half consenting, succeeds in spite of all in freeing herself from every form of particularism that would enslave her, as though by some divine instinct that warns and saves her. She steers her bark in the midst of peril, ever in danger of contamination, hindrance and immobilization. Yet always she tears herself from the mirage, rises above her foreboding and continues on her triumphant course towards new horizons, never allowing her destiny to be bound up with that of human systems or interests. For an impartial historian this is a moral miracle which constitutes convincing proof of the divine nature of the Church.

Christian antiquity

The first chapter of this book told of the laborious trans-planting of the frail Christian seedling from the soil of Jewish and oriental culture to that of the Greco-Roman world. The freeing of nascent Christianity from Judaism and all its past history that weighed her down was the first and essential condemnation of particularism, though such an uprooting from affective tradition and age-old mentality could not fail to be painful. And once she had taken root in Mediterranean and, later, Latin society and culture, Christianity was to ex-perience new dangers. These she avoided by immediately overflowing beyond the borders of the Roman Empire. She reached Egypt, North Africa, Persia, Arabia, Ethiopia and doubtless India also. Then the peoples of the Caucasus, the tribes of the Sahara, the barbarian clans wandering from the Danube to the steppes of Russia. When the Germanic inva-sions were let loose in A.D. 406, Christianity was ready, with its bishops and missionaries, to absorb them also.

Roman paganism never succeeded in mastering the new faith whose adherents were ready to pay for their liberty with their blood. Neither did the Church let herself be domi-nated by Christian Emperors and defended her liberty against the Caesaro-papalism of Justinian. Pope Vigilius boldly faced him, claiming for the Church freedom of faith and action.

Fustel de Coulanges wrote: "As regards government of the state, we may say that Christianity transformed it in its essence, precisely because it refused to be mixed up with it. In former times, religion and the state were one and the same. . . . But Jesus Christ broke this alliance that paganism and the Empire wished to renew; he declared that religion is not the same thing as the state and that obedience to Caesar is not the same thing as obedience to God."

Meanwhile, Christian missionaries were carrying the Gospel message to the limits of the Empire: St Patrick was preach-ing in Ireland, St Columba in Scotland, St Augustine of

Canterbury in England, the Englishman St Boniface became
the apostle of Germany, the Greeks Cyril and Methodius
those of the Slavs.

Then came the time for the Barbarians. Faced with the
general break up of the Roman Empire, certain Christians
were terrified and were inclined to confuse the end of a civilization with the end of the world. Others however, like St
Augustine and Salvian, could watch without fear the new
orders of Providence and denounced the sins of Christians
of the Roman Empire. The Church of those days broke away
from past ideas, made contact with the Barbarians, tamed
them, made them more human, and at the same time saved
what was valuable in both Christian and pagan antiquity.
Figures such as St Leo and St Gregory the Great act as a link
between the ancient world and the Middle Ages, and were
great stimulators of missionary zeal. The Roman Empire
could set no bounds to the Church either in time or space.
This had already been declared in the teaching of Irenaeus,
Tertullian and Origen.

The Middle Ages

Weakening of the central powers and the consequent public
insecurity led to the rise of the feudal system, a veritable
mosaic of minor princedoms, each practically independent
and sovereign, and frequently at war one with another. This
created a new danger for the Church, for ecclesiastics, like
the rest of the people, became vassals of their feudal lords
who arrogated to themselves the choice of bishops and abbots,
claiming the right to confer upon them their insignia of crozier
and ring, and nominating parish priests also. The German
Emperors, who alone were able to guarantee the security of
the Holy See, went so far as to try and control papal elections.
In spite of herself, the Church was in danger of becoming
subservient to local or imperial particularism.

Gregory VII rose up against these pretensions and freed

the Church from feudal claims. Henry IV, the excommuni-
cated Emperor of Germany, was obliged to go to Canossa
(January 1077). Although this submission was not maintained,
it did deliver the Church from laymen investing ecclesiastics
with the symbols of their ministry, the crozier and ring. One
hundred and fifty years later, the papacy gained a permanent
victory in this matter, under Innocent IV and the Council of
Lyons (1245). It was at this time also that St Thomas Becket
gave his life for the liberty of the Church. Philip the Fair of
France was the only sovereign who, under the inspiration of
his legal-minded counsellors, resisted the papacy successfully.

This was the time also when the Popes tried to circumvent
and penetrate the Mohammedan barrier by sending ambassa-
dors and missionaries far into Asia, notably the Franciscans
and Dominicans. Raymond Lull suggested new ways of
approaching Islam; and, in spite of their frequently sordid
side, the Crusades at least had the advantage of welding
Christianity together and by so doing to assure its peace. In
the face of newly rising nationalism in many lands, the Church
continued to affirm and maintain her traditional catholicity.

In the philosophical world, the auspicious liberty of the
schools guaranteed freedom from particularism and exclusivism. The Thomist synthesis is clearly acceptable to the Church
because of its depth of quality, its unifying harmony and its
teaching value which gave beginners, especially seminarists,
an intellectual training that was strict and orderly. This is
proved by the Thomist renaissance of the nineteenth century,
inspired by Leo XIII. But the Church has never proscribed
other ways of Christian thought, as is shown by the continuation of the Scotist tradition which maintains some of the
Augustinianism of St Bonaventure, and also the school of
Suarez in the sixteenth and following centuries. These schools
of thought suffice to show that though the Church may have
her preferences, she does not intend to impose one way of
thought to the exclusion of all others. In his *Catéchisme des*

Incroyants, Sertillanges, when speaking of the Church, asks the question:

> Is not the Church, with her Thomism, particularist in philosophy?
>
> [And he replies:] The Church favours Thomism because she judges this system of fundamental ideas more favourable to the intellectual welfare of believers and more in keeping with her dogma. It is her own particular philosophy just as plainchant is her own particular music; but she no more imposes Thomism as a universal obligation in philosophy than she imposes plainchant on all modern musicians. St Augustine was a Platonist, Fénelon a Cartesian, Malebranche made up his own philosophy; but all three and hundreds of others, although attached to this or that system, made profession both intellectually and practically of the same Christian faith.

Modern times

Other forms of particularism rose up and threatened the Church's universalism at the time of the Renaissance and the Reformation—particularism that triumphed to its own undoing in the heresies and schisms of Germany, Switzerland and England. These movements of secession and revolt ended in national churches, subject to political power and cut off henceforth from true universalism. They are the very antithesis of catholicity; none but the true Church could defend herself, at the cost of many efforts and struggles, against the invaders' hand and the constantly reviving forms of individualism.

As a compensation for these losses and an affirmation of her vitality, the Church, at that same period, accompanied explorers to newly-discovered or recently penetrated lands of America and the Far East. This led to certain compromising and confusing situations, but the Church would never subject herself wholly to the schemes of the conquerors, and nearly always protested against abuses and indolence, as is shown by the indignant protests of Las Casas. Moreover, by far the greater part of the Church's missionary sons have shone by their disinterestedness and the nobility of their charity: St Francis Xavier in the Far East, St Francis Solano and St Peter Claver in America, Ricci in China, Nobili in India, soon to be followed by the members of the *Missions Etrangères* (the Paris Foreign Missionary Society).

In the West, the Church had to defend herself against cramping and relentless doctrines that would have reduced her to a sect without object or scope. Gallicanism was a wound in the side of the Catholic Church, and Jansenism taught distressing ideas on predestination and the salvation of man, and so minimized sacramental teaching and practice that it has been called "Calvinism warmed up". It is well known how energetically the Church, in Rome and in France too, defended her catholic conception of things against these deforming "exclusivisms".

Other attacks were launched against the Church at the end of the eighteenth century: kings and rulers who wished to be the absolute masters of their national church. "Josephism", named after the Emperor Joseph II of Austria, was the outcome of a doctrine known as "Febronianism", systematized by a student of Canon van Espen, Professor of the Law Faculty at Louvain.

A sincere believer and penetrated by the influence of the French "philosophers", this Emperor, the friend of "the enlightened", claimed to regulate everything in the Church. Not only did he forbid bishops to refer to Rome cases of conscience reserved to the examination of the Pope and also certain dispensations for marriages, but he gave orders that the bishops' pastoral letters should be submitted for his approval. He changed diocesan boundaries at will. He replaced the diocesan seminaries by five "general seminaries", and suppressed a considerable number of religious houses. He regulated details of the liturgy, processions, the number of Masses to be said and even the number of candles to be lit at certain services. Frederick II, king of Prussia, who watched all this with a mocking eye, used to refer to him as "my brother the Sacristan" (Mgr Arquillière, *Histoire de l'Église*).

Pius VI made a special journey to Vienna to check these extravagant reforms, nevertheless the spirit of Josephism survived in Austria until the Concordat of 1855.

The present day

After the dark days of the French Revolution, another sovereign, Napoleon I, tried to bring the Church into line with his military ideas. Again the Church resisted, and although she agreed to the Concordat of 1801 with its lamentable Organic Articles, it was only on condition that her essential rights were safeguarded. The Church had no more intention of becoming an imperial Church than she had of becoming the servant of the Revolution. The gentle firmness of Pius VII enabled her to save what was essential and await better days.

The nineteenth century is particularly noteworthy for the prodigious expansion of missionary enterprise, emanating especially from France, and also for the Church's care to safeguard her liberty of action and her universalism. This explains the popes' tenacity in the matter of their temporal dominions, for which they only ceased to protest and to struggle when the Lateran Treaty assured them territorial independence despite the smallness of their sovereign territory. New forms of particularism were rising up to challenge the Church's catholicity. This time they were not only political in origin but also social, economic, racial or philosophical. Faced with the rise of capitalism, with the movement towards colonization, with nationalism, the Church's attitude is always the same: to defend herself against the spirit of sectarianism, never to allow herself to be enclosed within any human system or framework.

After the libertinism and indifference of the eighteenth century, the middle classes, sobered by the Revolution and brought back to the faith by religious romanticism, feeling the need of stability and the renewal of Christianity, were in danger of monopolizing the organization of the Church, at least in France, and of associating it too narrowly with their own social milieu. But the Church, while directing the return of the middle classes to the faith, did not forget the situation in which new economic conditions had placed the working classes. The work of socially-minded Catholics, relying on the doctrine of Leo XIII and the popes that followed him, has been to try to break the close connection between the middle classes and the Church, and to free her from an alliance that might do more harm than good. On the other hand, when the Catholic hierarchy sees generous-minded priests and laymen turn their attention to the working classes, she will not hear of the idea of a Church so "democratic" and "working class" that it loses its universal character. This was one of the questions at issue in the recent controversies about priest-workmen and the various modern youth movements.

Similarly, if the Church has welcomed European colonization of under-developed territories, because of the facilities that such colonies give to the furthering of the Gospel, she does not shut her eyes to the abuses of colonization, and has never ceased to protect the interests and the rights of native populations. More recently, through the voice of the bishops and the pope, she has reminded men of the right of every population to direct its own affairs progressively and under certain conditions. The Church wishes to remain the home of all peoples and classes of society, without subordinating her mode of action to the points of view of those in power, be they men or nations.

Last century witnessed a growing awareness among certain peoples of their rights, and this movement has become more widespread in our own days. The Church acknowledges the legitimacy of a certain nationalism, but against nationalistic excesses she defends not only her missionaries and her priests, but all Christians and all men because an exaggerated nationalism would be harmful to mutual peace and universal understanding, would injure the Catholic spirit, and impair the supra-nationalism of the Church.

Catholicity and modern dangers

We see, then, that all through history the Church has had to defend her catholicity, always threatened, sometimes compromised, but never denied. She has had to protect it against external influences: heretics and sectarians, political ascendancy, forces of every kind. She has never agreed to be the servant of the victors of the moment, be they princes like Justinian, Henry IV of Germany, Louis XIV, Joseph II of Austria or Napoleon, or nations at the height of their power, like Spain, Portugal, France and England, or in our days, Russia or the United States of America. If at one time she judged it prudent to fix the limits of Spanish and Portuguese influence in the world by the famous *Padroado*, she never agreed to this privilege being turned into a paralysing monopoly. The object of the foundation of the Congregation *de Propaganda Fide* in 1622 was to escape from the outworn control of the Portuguese crown over the missions.

The same act was intended to give back to ecclesiastical authority the guidance of religious institutes whose rights over missionary work had proved too great a burden in the problems of evangelization. The Church has every respect for diversity of minds and of nations, she calls upon the initiative and the dynamism of all, but she refuses to compromise her liberty, and remains mistress of her destiny and mother of all peoples. She was grateful to France for the protection she gave to the missions in China and the Near East, but this protection was only provisional and tactical, and the Church shook herself free of it the moment it became harmful and immobilizing. Nothing could be further from her thoughts than the sectarian spirit, whether it shows itself in the sociological or the religious order of things, or appears in matters liturgical, philosophical or even theological. The

Church's freedom, compared with all human systems and framework, is both the condition and the expression of her catholicity.

That the Church, in spite of the weight of years, the opposition of man, the faults and sins of her members which mount up with the passing of time and are never forgotten, should have succeeded in keeping to her course, maintaining her watchful alertness, her versatility, in the midst of so many difficulties, should fill even the most insignificant historian with wonder. It is a palpable proof of her divinity. Only the power of God could have saved her from sinking in the course of the centuries, could have preserved her essential features in the midst of so many apparent changes, could have maintained the harmony and the reality of her unity and her universal influence. For two thousand years she has kept to her road through empires, intrigues and persecutions; she has remained faithful to her universal ideal by her tangible presence in every epoch and every civilization. With the wisdom born of experience she has kept her youth and her energy. While welcoming all kinds of character, all forms of culture, all nations, she remains her true self, identical in all essentials with what she was on the day of Pentecost, in the time of Clovis or under Charlemagne. She passes through the ages and across continents without giving way to syncretism but embracing all she finds that is good, without obsequious submission to the great but making terms with them, without forgetting heaven but showing herself human and adaptable to all. While remaining transcendent, she is incarnate in history, and while showing herself truly human, she remains truly divine. She is indeed a historical miracle that the most subtle human intelligence cannot explain.

THE EASTERN CHURCHES

The existence and the renown of the Eastern Churches are a privileged witness to the catholicity of the Church. Without them, the Church would be almost entirely Latin and would seem to disown a considerable part of her past and of the world, the place of her origin and an important section of humanity. The exceptional and precious case of the Eastern Churches must therefore be considered here. But first we must note the diversity admitted and approved by the Church in the liturgical order, her "Catholic liturgy". Within this general outline, we shall then locate the Eastern Churches themselves, briefly describing their origin and history, their present situation, the significance of their existence and the abiding lessons that they offer us.

Catholic liturgy

Fr Dalmais in his *Initiation Théologique* (I, p. 101), after setting forth the liturgy as an action and a mystery, gives it the following definition: "the substance of those rites and formulas by which the priestly ministry of Christ, Mediator between God and man, is exercised in the Church for the fulfilment of the mystery of salvation."

Consequently, the liturgy is a social reality which develops according to different peoples and circumstances in various directions, combines into a whole the genius of divers nations and times, and which has been carefully handed down to us by past centuries. By the very fact of this diversity of language and ceremonial, the liturgy is a further manifestation of the Church's catholicity and her wonderful fertility.

Writing of the Eastern Christians in his book *L'Unité de l'Église* (p. 121), Abbé Quénet says:

> The Church has no intention of depriving Christian peoples (Easterns) of these admirable and ancient forms of prayer and sacrifice to which everything binds them: the past, the memory of their forefathers, their homeland, their own hearts. The Church has no wish to upset them in their faith by upsetting them in their rites. On the contrary, she delights in the wealth which these ancient and holy liturgies give her. . . . And what a wonderful and further witness to her catholicity they are!

Without a single exception, all the rites are to be found in the Church: the Byzantine rite, with Greek, Arabic, Slavonic, Rumanian and Georgian as its liturgical languages; the Armenian rite, with its Armenian language; the Syrian rite, with Syriac and Arabic for its languages; the Chaldean rite, with its own language; the Maronite rite, using Arabic and Syriac; the Coptic rite, using Coptic, Arabic and that ancient form of the Abyssinian tongue known as Ge'ez. The existence of all these peoples and rites prevents the Church from becoming simply the Church of the West, an exclusively Latin Church. They provide her with both geographical and liturgical catholicity of character.

This liturgical catholicity is shown not only by the Eastern rites but also by European rites other than the Latin. Without mentioning the Germanic elements that have become integrated in the Roman liturgy, the Council of Trent provided for the maintenance of liturgies more than two centuries old. To quote Fr Dalmais again (p. 122):

In this way, ancient usages were preserved by the monastic order, especially in the divine office. The Premonstratensians and the Dominicans safeguarded French usage of the eleventh to twelfth centuries; the Carmelites for a long time kept the rite used in the Church of the Holy Sepulchre at the time of the Crusades.[1] Many local churches, especially in France, Germany and England, might well have availed themselves of this decision. Henry VIII's schism excluded England once and for all. The untimely creation of neo-Gallican liturgies in France (seventeenth-eighteenth centuries) and the political and religious troubles in Germany rendered the Council's ruling sterile in the majority of cases. Towards the middle of the nineteenth century, the whole of France, under the influence of Dom Guéranger, returned to the Roman liturgy. Only the church of Lyons succeeded in preserving some of its ancient usages, which were moreover mostly authentically Roman and could trace their descent to Carolingian times. More recently,

[1] Mention should be made also of the Benedictines, whose Office is that laid down by St Benedict in his Rule in the sixth century, and differs considerably from the Roman Office. [*Trans.*]

an effort has been made to recover lost liturgical treasures, and a few dioceses in Normandy and the Rhineland have restored ancient usage.

To these may be added the use of Braga (Portugal), the Carthusian use (proper to the Carthusians only), the Mozarabic rite which is still celebrated in the cathedral at Toledo (and three times a year at Salamanca), and the Ambrosian rite at Milan. The Eastern liturgies, then, take their place within a greater whole which, as we have said, demonstrates the catholicity of the Church.

The rise and development of the Eastern Churches

To Europeans, the Christian East too often appears as a world largely medieval, troublesome and peculiar. Nevertheless, it bears witness to an enchanting past and, as Pierre Rondot shows in his admirable work *Les Chrétiens d'Orient*, it shows remarkable vitality today and may well be an active agent in the future of the world. We must now recall, therefore, how it came into being and how certain groups of Christians have preserved or recovered union with the Roman Church.

The schism of the Eastern Churches that became definitive in the eleventh century was not an isolated event but was the consequence and the ratification both of doctrinal divergencies and sociological and cultural differences, arising from the fact that the two parts of Christendom had developed in contrary directions for several centuries. At the moment when Rome was falling under the blows of the Barbarians in 476, Byzantium remained a living and prosperous metropolis, where the imperial and religious powers were closely united. Greek culture continued to shine at Constantinople when it was crumbling and dying in the Roman world. Byzantine ecclesiastical law, moreover, tended to recognize the autonomy of national Churches, while in the West power remained, at least in principle, strongly centralized. Over-excited by natural sensitiveness and enslaved to political influences, the conflicting parties no longer spoke the same language, no longer understood each other, became obdurate in their opinions, and finally the separation from the Mother Church was effected.

In this connection Fr Rondot writes:

> The Western Church was well able to cultivate the seeds of Christianity and to assure its harmonious development in the Greco-Roman world. But it could not impose its methods on Asia, or even maintain intellectual contact with her. There was a difference if not frank opposition between the destiny of Christians sprung from Western stock and those of the East. The Churches of Asia, violently separated from rigorous Roman discipline, were bound up with the lot of exaggerated empires that rose to power quickly and as quickly were abolished. In the kind of wasteland that religious and civil quarrels had produced on the outskirts of the Empire, Islam was to find room for surprisingly instantaneous development (seventh century).

Thus it was that Eastern Christians constantly found themselves surrounded, drowned, swallowed up by Mohammedan hordes; while Catholic minorities were themselves usually surrounded by schismatic peoples, incorrectly called Orthodox. These facts must not be forgotten if we are to understand the tenacious fidelity shown by these Christians in their determination to exist all through the centuries, a fidelity even more intense among the Catholics who were usually in a minority.

Since we cannot here retrace the history, or even describe in detail the present situation of these various Christian bodies in communion with Rome, we must be content to recall the destiny or the names of a few of them. Allowing a just margin for error necessary in such matters, Fr Janin reckons that the dissident Churches number $176\frac{1}{2}$ million adherents and the Catholic communities rather more than 10 million. Among these, the most important historically is the Maronite community (885,000 members in Lebanon or dispersed throughout the world), the most important numerically is the group of uniat churches of the Byzantine rite (7½ million members). There are 180,000 Catholics of the Armenian rite; 170,000 of the Syrian rite; 1,220,000 of the Chaldean rite; and 125,000 of the Coptic rite.

By way of example, we give a brief outline of the Maronite community. These Christians trace their descent from St Maro, a saintly solitary who died before A.D. 423. It seems that at first they favoured the Monothelite heresy, which taught that in our Lord there was but one will, the divine will. But they were reconciled to Rome first in the twelfth century and finally in the sixteenth, since when, in the fastnesses of the Lebanon mountains, they have preserved intact the Catholic faith, in spite of persecutions, especially by the Turks. They have a Patriarch, two metropolitan archbishops and eight episcopal dioceses. The religious life has always been held in great esteem among them, and in the Near East they constitute an important centre for the spread of the Catholic faith. "Among the Christians of the East", says Fr Rondot, "those of Lebanon are the most fortunate, having matured gradually through history."

Spiritual and liturgical riches of the Eastern Churches

The position of Catholics of the Eastern rites in the Church is based not only on the hope inspired by their permanence in a schismatic or Mohammedan world, but also on the treasures found in their liturgical and cultural tradition. The loss of these treasures would be for the Church a grave impairment of her catholicity, a retreat entailing incalculable consequences.

Abbé Calvet, in *Le Problème Catholique de l'Union des Églises*, says:

> We must never forget what we owe to the East: the beginning of the Gospel and faith in Jesus Christ; the beginning of the liturgy; monastic life. We are their debtors also for many great doctors and saints: St John the Evangelist, St Athanasius,

St John Chrysostom, St Basil, St Gregory Nazianzen, St Polycarp and St Irenaeus who brought the Gospel to Lyons, besides the Solitaries of the Thebaid who caused holiness to flourish in the desert. The East preserves these great memories in her sanctuaries, and causes them to live in a liturgy whose splendour and brilliance surpasses our own. It was in the East that Jesus lived and watered the earth with his precious blood, and the Eastern Christians guard these sacred places as well as those sanctified by the first apostles. The East is the inheritor of St Paul's field of labour. These material facts, these places that join us to our origins, to Jesus himself, they are there, in that Eastern world that has known so much subversion, so much suffering. It is not possible that so much greatness, so much beauty, such religious wealth, should remain outside Catholic unity. It is for the West to stretch out her hand to touch these sacred relics and to embrace them in her unity.

Those who have been present at Eastern ceremonies and have meditated on their liturgical texts and the writings of the Eastern Fathers, will bear witness to the deep impression made by them; an impression of entering into a region that is purely and most highly religious, a really sacred realm. God appears there in all his glory and the liturgy is a foretaste of heaven. Nothing is too beautiful, nothing too noble for the worship of the King of kings, and the heavenly host seems to us very near and at the same time remote. The majesty of the rites, the full and solemn splendour of the chant, the depth of the formulas used are without comparison. Eyes and heart find there their pasture and mortals are drawn into a heavenly world. As Gogol says: "In a certain sense, the divine liturgy is the permanent reproduction of a sublime excess of love accomplished on our behalf."

The priestly gestures, the glitter of the gold and colours, the richness of vocabulary and the quality of the reverence turn this liturgy into food for the religious soul.

As an example, we quote a prayer of St Metrophanes of Smyrna, to which St Pius X attached indulgences:

In glorifying thee now, O Trinity, unique Principle, Ruler and Creator of all things, sovereign Nature, eternal, lifegiving, compassionate friend of mankind, Goodness itself, we beg of thee pardon for our sins, peace for the world, concord for the Churches. O unique Power, sole divine Sovereignty, graciously welcome to thy threefold splendour, thy threefold glory, those who worship thee with holy song; deliver them from their sins, from temptation and from adversity, and in thy mercy grant speedily to the Churches both peace and union. O Christ, my Saviour, who didst dwell in the womb of the Virgin and who didst appear in this world, thine own handiwork, as both God and man, without change or mixture; thou who didst faithfully promise to be ever with thy servants, grant by the intercession of her who was thy Mother, peace to thy whole flock.

The principal features of Eastern spirituality are seen in this one quotation: depth of theological content, emphasis on the principal dogmas of our faith (Blessed Trinity, Incarnation; though mention of the Resurrection is wanting), mode of expression that is both human and divine, conspicuous place of the Blessed Virgin, quality of religious feeling. . . .

The writings of the Eastern Fathers as well as translations of Eastern liturgical prayers have been brought within reach of all in recent years (see bibliography at end of book).

The Holy See and the Eastern Churches

After this, we shall not be surprised to learn that the popes, more especially the popes of modern times, have frequently expressed their esteem and veneration for these liturgical riches which are both an adornment and a witness to the Church's catholicity. It would be impossible to quote the innumerable documents published about them. A few examples only must suffice to demonstrate this marked papal interest.

In his encyclical *Praeclara gratulationis* (1894), Leo XIII extolled the Eastern Churches by speaking of "the East, cradle of salvation for the human race" and "the Eastern

Churches, illustrious for the faith of their forefathers and their ancient glories. . . . Frequently when vindicating the Catholic faith, we use quotations and arguments drawn from the doctrine, the usages and the rites of the Eastern Churches".

On May 1st, 1917, in the *Motu proprio, Dei providentis*, instituting the Congregation for the Eastern Church, Benedict XV said:

> In our fatherly love, we embrace all particular Churches, but especially the eastern Churches. For indeed their greater antiquity shines with such great brilliance of holiness and sound doctrine that even today, after so many centuries, we see its light shedding lustre over the whole of Christendom. . . . This present *Motu proprio* will make it more evident that the Church of Jesus Christ, because it is neither Latin, nor Greek, nor Slav, but Catholic, makes no difference between her sons, and that they all, be they Greeks, Latins, Slavs or of any other nation, occupy the same rank before the Apostolic See.

A few months later, this same pope founded in Rome the Pontifical Institute for Eastern Studies, which was to be open "both for Uniat Eastern Churches and those called Orthodox".

Pius XI and Pius XII seized every opportunity to praise the Eastern Churches and to specify the irenical methods required in treating with dissidents, as well as the respect and esteem due to Eastern rites and forms of piety, e.g. on the occasion of the tricentenary of the martyrdom of St Josaphat (1923), the solemnities commemorating the Council of Nicaea (1925), the encyclical *Rerum orientalium* (1928), on the fifteenth centenary of the death of St Cyril of Alexandria (1944), the letter to Ukranian Catholics (1945) etc. It would be well also to include a quotation from Pius XI, March 25th, 1938, in which he protests against untimely attempts in the past to Latinize the East:

> In an exaggerated devotion to unity and concord, and lack-ing the needful instruction as to the conditions and character of followers of Oriental rites, certain zealots have attempted

to corrupt these sacred rites or to induce those who use them to adopt the Latin rite. But the Roman Pontiffs have resisted such attempts with all their might, sparing no pains in the matter. . . . When they realized that certain people were trying to convert the Easterns from the use of their own rites, or were seeking to introduce certain changes, they condemned these inopportune efforts, declaring that they wished these Eastern rites to be maintained in their integrity. For the Roman Pontiffs hold that liturgical diversity, born of the particular mentality of various peoples, far from lessening the unity of our holy faith and sacred worship, is rather a recommendation and an adornment for this unity. For it enables people to understand more easily that the one and only Catholic religion corresponds perfectly with the nature and customs of all peoples, and brings forth abundant and varied fruits in all their beauty (Motu proprio *Sancta Dei Ecclesia*).

The "conversion" of Latin Catholics

"We lay a special injunction upon you, convert the Latins." So spoke Pius XI in May 1934 to some newly-ordained priests of the Eastern rite. The "conversion" was to be an esteem and love of Eastern liturgies, since they are an irreplaceable sign of the Church's catholicity. A few years earlier he had deplored the fact that the Eastern schisms had resulted not only primarily in the lamentable ignorance and mutual distrust of peoples for one another, but also in prejudices consequent on long standing animosity. In the same document (*Rerum orientalium*), he insisted that seminarists should be more adequately instructed on all that concerns Eastern rites. In this way "they will become more conscious of the love they owe to the true Spouse of Christ, whose wondrous beauty and unity in the diversity of rites will shine more brightly in their eyes". It is high time, he said on another occasion, that misunderstandings should cease.

For indeed we have much to learn from Eastern Christians. We must know them and love them not only because they are our brethren and a long standing fidelity makes them worthy of our admiration, but also because familiarity with their liturgy, their piety and their doctrine will prove a useful counterbalance to the excesses and possible deviations of our Western Christianity. In the West, there is perhaps a danger of forgetting, or at least becoming insufficiently aware of God's presence and greatness, the importance of worship and of service both bodily and social, the desirability of devotion to our Lady founded on theology, the importance of Christ's resurrection in our faith, the fact that the Church is not limited to what is Latin or Western or Mediterranean, the primacy of contemplation, the sense of tradition and realistic fidelity to the past, etc. Considerations such as these are most evidently in keeping with the mentality and the history of the Eastern Churches—considerations of which they can remind us and by means of which we should be inspired, for they are an essential element in Christian revelation. A reflection by Fr Bourgeois S.J. may well be applied more generally to other forms of culture: "If Catholicism is necessary for Russian culture, there is a certain sense in which the deep religious spirit, the religious tragedy, expressed so powerfully by that culture, is necessary for the Church, so that on her human side she can better represent the balance of cultures that make up the human race."

Through the embodiment of revelation in Eastern cultures and liturgies, the Church manifests her catholicity more clearly. Catholics of the Latin rite should have it at heart to show a more active interest in the Christian wealth of the East and to avoid any tendency towards narrow uniformity in the Church, as would be shown by the Latinization of their Eastern brethren. We need the East just as the East needs us. The Church, said Pius XII, does not belong to the West more than to the East.

Proof by opposites

A regrettable "counter-proof" of the Church's catholicity is provided for us in the history of dissident Churches and confessions. For them, the break with the Mother Church has been the sign for enslavement to some form of particularism, political, national, cultural or ritual. The powerful contemporary ecumenical movement cannot compensate for the tendency to crumble and disperse. History is there to remind us that all dissident Christian bodies have devoted themselves to the missionary apostolate very late and only on a small scale, and that they have always lacked a real universalist spirit and outlook. The analysis of the destiny of each of these Christian bodies would reveal these various forms of particularism. Here we can only give a few examples.

As regards the so-called Eastern Orthodox Churches, the Patriarch of Constantinople, in spite of his title of "Ecumenical Patriarch", has no jurisdiction in the real sense. Each of these Churches is independent of the rest; each is generally of the autocephalus or national type. And this leads to further divisions and independencies when national frontiers are modified by peace treaties. In these circumstances, it is easy to understand the tendency to political subjection or nationalistic particularism. In Russia, the Soviet government, heir to imperial domination, tries to make use of the Church to further her national and pro-Slav policy. This cramping process seems to have succeeded only too well, even if there are still many religious souls who continue to pray and worship God fervently within these narrow limits. Communist China similarly would like a Church that was both "Catholic" and "national". A Catholic apostle of the ecumenical movement, while elsewhere proclaiming the real value of the dissident Eastern Churches, has to admit their divisions, their not infrequent mutual opposition, their particularism: "The nationalistic principle", he says, "seems here to speak more forcefully than the genuine Christian principle of unity, both external and internal, of the people of God which is the Church." And once again he mentions their excessive conservatism, the almost total absence of adaptability, the lack of Christian activity in the world at large, their deficient missionary zeal.

The Church of England, or the Anglican Church, whose missionary expansion was late in coming but is now considerable, experiences analogous embarrassments due to the numerous parties and "points of view" among her members and her too rigorous attachment to political power. Her rigid connection with the British temperament as well as her insularity exclude any pretensions towards universalism, and is also responsible for the ever-increasing dissatisfaction with this official religion seen among many of her adherents. The Protestant reformers succeeded only in liberating the faith from what they called the autocracy and tyranny of Rome in order to subject it to the far more rigorous and rigid ascendancy of princes and states. The Protestant sects are the dreamed of prey of every form of particularism, national, political, cultural, dogmatic, even personal. History thus shows that Roman unity was the best safeguard for catholicity and indispensable liberty. To wish to rid oneself of God and of his lawful representatives, whatever their faults, always leads to self-condemnation to some form of man-made bondage. Nothing but a certain centralization of spiritual authority can save religion from temporal encroachments. Catholicity can only be preserved by wholehearted attachment to Christ and the unity of his one true Church.

THE UNIVERSAL APPROPRIATENESS OF CATHOLICISM

What has been said about the Eastern Churches effects the transition between the first division and the present division of this chapter. We have established the fact that historically the Church has rejected and excluded all particularism, but this only gives us a negative aspect of catholicity. In treating of the Eastern Churches we were already approaching the positive aspect, but at the same time we showed by the very diversity of recognized liturgies, of races and cultures affected, that the Church also excluded by this fact both racial and national particularism. Here, our intention is to enlarge upon the positive aspect of the question and show catholicity in action. The Catholic faith is appropriate and adaptable to all epochs, all nations, all ages, all conditions, all mentalities. This follows from the twofold basis of catholicity that we considered, following Fr Congar, in the preceding chapter: the universalism of Christ and the universalism of man, or, to put it in another way, divine totality and human totality, going forth to meet each other to form the Mystical Body of Christ. Such a consideration lends itself to limitless development, but the bounds set upon this work oblige us to do no more than sketch its main outlines.

For all epochs and all nations

Christianity overflows the centuries and fills all human space. It evolves while always remaining itself. It develops like a living being, yet loses nothing of its unity nor alters its essence. In every age it responds to the aspirations of the men of the time. And so we see it successively copying yet at the same time sublimating the structure of the Roman Empire, organizing and pacifying the ages of chivalry, preparing for the birth of the Western world and serving in certain respects as the vehicle or the framework for the spread of its civilization through the world. We see it controlling and satisfying the aspirations of men of the Renaissance, fashioning and underlying the successes of the Spanish and French *grands siècles*, building up the ruins brought about by the French Revolution and contributing its share to the formation of the modern world, grasping new techniques, new sciences, new forms of civilization. The man of the sixteenth or the twentieth century is as much at ease in Christianity as were those of the first or second. To every age the Christian faith brings light, appeases it with its orderliness and superior wisdom. It would be absurd, as Fr Sertillanges says, to ask religion for solutions of problems that concern simply human techniques and experience; but if the Church does not open any doors in matters concerning the temporal order, she provides all the keys, that is, the religious and moral principles for their solution.

Until the end of time, the Church will be there to counsel and guide, to purify and enliven, to enkindle and to bear. She dominates time, because she is both of heaven and of earth. With her eyes fixed on eternity, she embraces in her care all temporal and concrete conditions. Nothing human is foreign to her. She appeals to all men, whatever their economic or social environment. To all, she gives the words of life and salvation, received from him who, although he became man, ever remains the Lord of ages and the God of eternity.

The missionary history of the Church clearly shows her adaptability to all races, all continents, all nations. In her liturgy and her art, in her traditions and the forming of her doctrine, naturally enough she includes Jewish elements, but also elements that are of pagan origin. In a certain respect, she has copied her organization from that of the Roman Empire, has preserved and made fruitful the philosophical intuitions of Socrates, Plato and Aristotle, borrowed from both Barbarians and the Byzantine Roman Empire, but always remains herself, thoroughly digesting all elements drawn from external sources. In her laws, her ceremonies, her festivals and her devotions, she makes use of local customs after purifying them and "baptizing" them. "This adaptation of pagan customs", says Fr Sertillanges in *Le Miracle de l'Église*, p. 183, "prudently regulated, allows for the utilization of instincts and sentiments that preserve local traditions, and so lends powerful aid to the furthering of the Gospel. . . . The Church's cultus of saints and martyrs is a helpful substitute and replaces popular divinities in the minds of the populace."

The wonderful thing is that this attitude is concerned not only with the ancient world and Jewish or Greco-Roman civilizations, where Christianity first saw the day. Saints Cyril and Methodius proved the strength of this method of adaptation among the Slavs, Ricci among the Chinese, Nobili and his successors in India and missionaries such as Fathers Aupiais and Tempels in Africa. The fundamental doctrine of this matter was clearly formulated in an instruction of 1659 addressed by the Congregation for the Propagation of the Faith to the first Vicars Apostolic for the Far East. It can be considered as the charter for modern missions.

> Be careful to refrain from every inclination or suggestion to these people requiring them to change their rites, their customs and their manners, provided they are not manifestly contrary to true religion and sound morals. Indeed, what could be more absurd than to introduce France or Spain or Italy or any other European country into China? It is not European culture that you have to introduce, but the Faith which neither spurns nor harms these traditional rites and customs, provided they are not wicked, but rather seeks to preserve them.

The faith, then, is not bound up with Western civilization, but can be adapted to all peoples, nations and cultures. We see an illustration of this aspect of catholicity in the diversity of mentality found among Christians, both those of the present day and of future generations. Within the Catholic Church there are ways of thought and of piety that are specifically Italian, Spanish, French, German, American, etc. We may suppose and wish that the world of tomorrow will see influences in art, in literature, in theological thought, springing from other temperaments and traditions, Indian, Japanese, Chinese, African. In this respect, Catholicism has an immense career ahead of it in years to come. As Fr Sertillanges says again:

> The Gospel has barely started, but time is before it. . . . Our Church is progressive precisely because she is apostolic. If we look back from our days to those of the apostles, we

see her coming. If we look forward from the days of the
apostles to our own, we see her going. And to imagine that
she travels through time like a cart laden with unchangeable
baggage, would show great ignorance of her nature, and falsify
that note of apostolicity that we have shown as the authentic
fruit of a seed (*L'Église*).

For all circumstances and all mentalities

The Fathers of the Church and spiritual writers delight in
the idea that, in the Christian, Christ sanctifies each stage of
life, each social condition, each circumstance and concrete
attitude. It is indeed a wonderful thing that Christianity
should be appropriate to every age, every situation, every
mentality, with such infinite variety. This is a further manifestation of the Church's marvellous catholicity. Fr Sertillanges writes:

> A doctrine of life must adapt itself to every legitimate indi-
> vidual peculiarity, every aptitude, every form of moral tem-
> perament, all states of life, all professions. Without this, its
> fundamental message and, even more, its methods of action
> will have nothing concrete about them; it would be no more
> than a scheme without any practical utility. Of course every
> Christian should know himself to be a son of Christ, a bene-
> ficiary of his salvation, invited by him to live in conformity
> with the law of love and all its general consequences. But at
> the same time he will be aware of a "vocation", of "calls", of
> a personal ideal, of "social obligations", of "graces of state",
> and also of "actual graces" which are nothing else than graces
> of action, grace for each action and taking that action's form;
> so that he will know that he himself is referred to in the
> singularity of his case and of his person (*Catéchisme des
> Incroyants*).

And Fr Sertillanges adds that such diversity of application
of the doctrine was already the basis of the teaching of St John
the Baptist and of Jesus himself, emerging finally in the infinite variety of the saints and the various motives of
conversion:

. . . Strictly religious reasons, social reasons, political reasons, aesthetic reasons, sentimental reasons, that can be perceived at work during a process that contrives to go beyond them all. Each individual has sought his own adaptation, and finding it receives the impression that the Church had been made for the express purpose of providing for his needs. But another has approached the truth by a different way, a third by still another, and all together prove its integrity and its perfection.

We have already noted that piety varies in manner of expression according to national temperaments, but it takes on shades and special forms with individuals also. In one sense there are as many forms of Christianity as there are individual Christians, and yet it is the same Christianity always, experienced differently and expressed individually by each person. Such is the wonderful fecundity of the true faith, diversity in unity which is the mark of the divine presence and of the multiform action of the One Spirit. A poor old woman, a learned professor, a child, a workman, each will envisage Christianity from a different angle. Their prayer, their faith, their union with God will be personal. But all will be at ease, all will feel at home in the Catholic Church, the city of the faithful and the mother of all the living. This variety of vocation is shown again in the extraordinary expansion of religious congregations, of forms of piety and the practice of prayer, in the thousand and one ways of going to God without ever forsaking Catholic unity. Thus the Church appears as the richest and most gifted of human assemblies. In her there dwells the fullness of humanity because first of all there dwells in her the fullness of divinity.

Human fullness and divine fullness

And so the Church goes on her way, gathering up all that is good, just and holy, integrating all, assimilating all, setting her mark on all that all may pay homage to the true God, the God of all living things. As a consequence, she is the harmonious meeting-place of the most contradictory and apparently incompatible elements, races, nations, physical and psychological temperaments, divergent and contrary ideas, tendencies of all kinds, values from pagan sources. "The Church alone," says Newman, "has succeeded in casting out what was bad and retaining what was good, and in bringing into the unity of her synthesis elements that in all other spheres are incompatible."

A passage from Harnack, quoted in Sertillanges' *Le Miracle de l'Église*, falls into place here:

> From the beginning, the Christian religion has shown itself to possess a character of universality in virtue of which it has set its seal upon the whole of life, with all its occupations, height, depth, feelings, thoughts and actions. Sin and defilement alone have been set aside. It has built itself up with everything capable of life, owing to its genius for organization. It has broken down everything outside itself, and has preserved all that it contained within itself. This has been possible (though ignored or unknown by all, yet realized by every Christian soul) because considered in its essence the Christian religion is something simple or, more truly, universal, Catholic, able to unite itself with every coefficient and seeking to do so. While remaining exclusive it attracts to itself every foreign element of any value. By this sign it has conquered, for over all that is human—eternal or transitory—it has placed the cross and so has subjected all to the next world.

Commenting on this, Fr Sertillanges says: "The Church is a seed which develops at the expense of its surroundings, living on those surroundings without belonging to them. Refusal to compromise and flexibility are her two complementary characteristics. . . . She absorbs and is not absorbed."

Elsewhere the same writer says that Catholic doctrine is a universal relationship and a universal paradox. It reunites all things and brings all things to their fullness without discord. It is throughout space and is as far from mediocrity as from partiality for any extreme. In it contraries meet and are each in their turn admitted:

> At bottom it is optimistic and pessimistic according to the point of view from which it is regarded. It exalts both mystic-

ism and objectivity, austerity and joy, virginity and love, self-concern and generous sacrifice, suffering and happiness, freedom and subordination, equality and hierarchy, peace and just war, gentleness and firmness, prudence and ready confidence, abandonment to Providence and work, faith and good works, free will and grace, detachment and ardour of life, mercy and justice, pity and patient goodness in all the stages of man's time of trial on earth, and the necessary sternness of the last judgement (*Catéchisme des Incroyants*).

The Catholic Church is therefore universal at all levels and from all aspects. Vessel of the whole truth, she appears in history as the answer to all situations and all conditions, satisfying all men and all races, as appropriate for Easterns as for Westerns, on all sides unfolding her fecundity and her holiness, and in an admirable manner preserving herself from all particularism. No human institution could prove itself of such permanence and such flexibility. To preserve her from falling into the million snares on her way, a divine hand was required to guide her, she had herself to be divine, like the shadow of him who is the Master of mankind and the Master of all time.

CHAPTER IV

THE CATHOLICITY OF THE CHURCH IN THE MODERN WORLD

History has shown us the Church defending and spreading her catholicity everywhere, keeping herself free from all particularism and welcoming humanity in its fullness. She stretches forth her hand to the East as to the West, and out of the infinite variety of human values she forms a greater unity in Christ. The present chapter will continue and complete this inquiry by applying it to the twentieth century. First we shall note contemporary progress in the general idea of human unity and then we shall set out the Church's answer, under the last three popes, to this aspiration of men of today. The intention, therefore, is to portray catholicity in action in the modern world. In general, the Church has to justify herself in the face of one of the gravest charges ever made against her. She has to meet firmly the most biting defiance which finds expression in some words of Jean Schlumberger: "Christianity must recognize that there are certain great religions which it cannot penetrate. All over the world spheres of influence have been allotted, definite positions taken up. . . . To leave one system of belief in order to enter another is a change of civilization rather than religion. Ultimately Christianity will have to accept this proof that it is linked with a culture and ways of thought that are not universal" (quoted in de Lubac, *Catholicism*, Eng. trans., p. 154).

In an age when humanity painfully seeks its unity, in a world more fully explored and brought into subjection, the Church affirms by life itself her catholicity and her cosmic outlook.

The twentieth century and the unity of the world

By a strange paradox, the age in which we live shows us, at one and the same time, men fighting one another in nationalistic or imperialistic wars or ideological conflicts, who manifest nevertheless a deep nostalgia, a veritable longing for world unity. People and civilizations feel increasingly their common solidarity and their interdependence. The speeding up of means of communication and the development of international exchange have, as it were, narrowed down the universe. As Valéry said, the age of a completed world is beginning—a world fully explored and circumscribed. And more than ever before, philosophical ideas and the most varied cultural expressions circulate throughout the world. National diversities and oppositions are accentuated, and yet at the same time ideas have a wider horizon, and men's interests are worldwide and extend even into inter-planetary space. Stumblingly and painfully humanity progresses towards unity.

Of this obvious and irreversible phenomenon, we would like to cite one or two of the harbingers and signs, coming from the most divers horizons: Whitman, Claudel, Ségalen and Fr Teilhard de Chardin. Four poets, we might almost say four cantors of the cosmos, of which only two make explicit claim to be Catholics. It must be admitted that Walt Whitman (1819–92), an American poet and democrat, belongs entirely to last century; he is mentioned here, however, because of the inferential and prophetic character of his work, tinged with a kind of cosmic and naturalistic universalism. His is a pagan song of confidence in life, typically American, moreover, where the sap of vegetation is mixed with the din of factories, human brotherhood with the variety of the world's races:

> In me the caresser of life wherever moving,
>   backward as well as forward sluing,
> To niches aside and junior bending,
>   not a person or object missing,
> Absorbing all to myself and for this song . . .
>
> *(Song of Myself)*

With Claudel we enter a wholly different world, specifically religious and Christian, where the idea of the presence and the glory of God unite and colour all visions and give them perfection of proportion. In his old age, Claudel wrote to Jacques Madaule: "You must have recognized the general idea of my vocation, a great desire and a great urge towards divine joy, and an attempt to harness the whole world to this end, the world of feelings, the world of ideas, that of peoples and countrysides, to recall the entire universe to its original task in Paradise. . . ."

Can one conceive a broader intention, a poetic world more "catholic", a horizon more cosmic?

Claudel did not waste the opportunities given him by his many journeys as consul or ambassador in China, Japan, in North and South America and in Belgium, but, like the discoverer of America whose fame he celebrated, he made himself "God's 'musterer' of the world". Everything interested him and everybody was charmed by him: the Japanese *Nô*, the turbid plains of China, the sea, the creations and discoveries of modern man, human loves, the piety of all kinds of people, history, space, the whole exterior cosmos and also that other world which is man of all continents. He bears witness to an age that seeks to embrace all things, reunite all things, unify all things, explain all things.

A few passages, chosen from among thousands, must suffice to show the manner and mind of the poet. So we find him writing:

Placed as we are between the world and God, it is for us to go to the aid of both, we must help them to reunite, no more simply by faith and the memory of man's Fall, but by the possession of Pentecost and Easter. It is for us to carry far and wide the orderliness, the prudence, the fruitfulness of the Faith. Nature, to its very depths, must be made to understand this order of things that we bring to it from its Creator. The Redeeming Word must make himself heard by all that the Creating Word has raised up, nothing should be a stranger to his revelation in glory. Before high Mass starts, all the aisles must be cleared, so that the priest may freely pass from one end of the church to the other, sprinkling all with the waters of sanctification as he goes, while the children of God intone the *Vidi aquam* and the *Asperges*.

His manner of expressing human and Christian solidarity is unequalled:

Not one of our brothers, even though he should wish it, is not of our company, for in the most pitiless miser, deep down in the heart of the prostitute and the filthiest drunkard, there is an immortal soul quietly and piously breathing, and which, because excluded from the light of day, practises nocturnal adoration. I hear those who speak when we are speaking and who weep when I kneel to pray. I accept all! I take them all to my heart, I understand them all, I need them every one and cannot do without them. There are many stars in the sky and their number exceeds my ability to count them, yet there is not one that is not necessary to me for the worship of God. There are millions of living beings and it is with difficulty that we see a few of them shining, while the others writhe in chaos and the vortex of sombre mire; there are millions of souls, but not a single one with whom I am not in communion through that sacred centre within it that murmurs *Pater Noster*.

From these pure Christian heights, rugged and implacable, we come down to earth again with that strange being Victor Ségalen, who today enjoys a revival through a new edition of his works. Born in Brittany and destined to die young, he was a naval doctor, an explorer and a poet. He knew Claudel, and although the composition of his poetry and prose differs from that of the Christian poet, like him he has a taste for open spaces, a sense of observation and understanding, a love for beautiful language, evocatory and lively. René Lalou says of him, "As a poet he reveals himself most in his book of Chinese *Steles*, which are like enduring crystallizations of 'back-waters filled with the raptures of the great river Diversity', rich images of 'life sweet to taste and sharp with spices'. Ségalen wanted to fix and to preserve, in his often hieratic or even hermetic descriptions, those beauties which a technically minded civilization seeking to reduce all things to a rigid uniformity is inclined to abolish. In the course of his short life, he showed for the changing and varied face of the universe an interest that was at least aesthetic and human."

All this was of absorbing interest to Fr Teilhard de Chardin also, but with how much besides! If he had a passion for the story of life and of the mind, it was not only as a scholar or a poet-philosopher, but as a Christian and a priest. We cannot here sketch the main lines of his ideas or even state those reservations demanded by thought still seeking and which must be judged as such. We shall only consider Teilhard as the witness of an age athirst for universalism and unity. His works speak of human "planetization", of "homogenization", of "universalization" and union. For an example of his style, we quote an article entitled "La Messe sur le monde" (the Mass over the world), which appeared in part in *La Table Ronde* (June 1955). One readily thinks of certain thoughts of Claudel on an analogous theme.

On the altar of the whole world, I, thy priest, will offer thee the work and the suffering of the world. . . . My chalice and my paten are those depths of a soul wide open to all the forces that, in an instant, will rise up from all corners of the globe and converge upon the Spirit. . . . I call upon all those, without a single exception, whose anonymous company forms the innumerable mass of the living: those who surround me and support me without my knowing them; those who come and those who go away; those especially who, in truth or through the fog of error, at their desks, in their laboratories or their factories, believe in the progress of things, and who today will passionately follow after the light. That surging multitude, vague or distinct, whose immensity terrifies us, this human ocean, whose slow and monotonous waves trouble the hearts of the most fervent believers. Would that at this moment my whole being might resound with its deep murmurings. Everything that will grow in the world during this day, everything that will diminish, everything that will die also: This, Lord, is what I strive to gather up in myself to offer it to thee; this is the matter of my sacrifice. . . . I will call down fire on all that, in human flesh, is ready to be born or to perish under the rising sun. . . .

Thus our age, whose aspirations we have heard expressed by a few great voices, relentlessly pursues the incomparable dream of its unity and recognizes the close solidarity that unites living men. Christians are preoccupied with the great tasks of ecumenism, and have learned to see the world again with the eyes of St Paul and of Christ; a world made one by the Cross and bathed in the light of Easter. All human beings feel at least vaguely that only wide horizons are permissible for them, and would say with General Smuts that a problem that is not stated in world-wide terms is a problem badly stated. The Church feels more than ever before her duty of bringing to these tangled aspirations the answer of her catholicity. She does not fail to do so, and causes her universalist character to shine forth with a splendour and veracity that former centuries never knew.

Benedict XV and deliverance from nationalism

To be accurate, we must go back to the pontificate of Leo XIII to see the Church becoming aware of the true dimensions of the modern world. He not only drew the attention of Christians to the working classes and social problems, but spoke as the teacher of faith and morals to the whole world, and consecrated that world to the Sacred Heart of Jesus at the dawn of the new century. Anybody who undertook to write the history of Catholic Missions would easily recognize in his work the outline of his successors' teaching in this regard: need of a local clergy, civilizing duty of missionaries, care for the unity of all Christians. He is the first pope to hold a central and essential place in the evolution of the present-day world.

After the pontificate of St Pius X, whose chief concern was to defend, reform and reorganize the Church in view of the gigantic onslaughts that she was about to suffer, the first world war broke out, a melancholy inheritance for his successor, Benedict XV. The new pope realized that it was for him to save Christians from the individualism of an excessive nationalism. He did this in various ways: by his intervention for the modifying and ending of the war, by inviting Christians to participate in the ecumenical movement (July 4th, 1918) and by calling upon them to cooperate in missionary work.

Such was the object of the Apostolic Letter *Maximum illud* (1919), the preparation and execution of which was confided to the intrepid Prefect of the Congregation for the Propagation of the Faith, Cardinal van Rossum. The importance of this letter cannot be exaggerated. It was the signal for the contemporary missionary revival and one of the most beautiful expressions of the Church's catholicity in the twentieth century. First he traces the history of the missions in the past and then goes on to consider the magnitude of what remains to be done. He stirs up the zeal of the heads of missions, urges them forward relentlessly, calls for the collaboration of other institutes and nations to form and organize a native clergy and commands missionaries to flee all appearance of nationalism.

Never lose sight of the importance and greatness of the vocation to which you have sacrificed yourselves. The mission confided to you is a truly divine mission which far surpasses the pettiness of human interests. . . . Realize that it is to each one of you that God says: "Forget thy people and the house of thy father" (Ps. 44. 2), and remember that you have to labour for the spread, not of some man-made kingdom, but the kingdom of Christ; not to gather recruits to be subjected to some earthly nation, but for the kingdom of heaven. Would it not be a really terrible thing for missionaries to give the impression of forgetting their dignity by busying themselves more about the affairs of their earthly fatherland instead of their heavenly fatherland, taking more care than they should to spread its power and glory above all else? Would not this be a fatal plague for the apostolate, destroying in the heart of the missionary the source of his love for souls, and enfeebling his influence over the greater part of his flock? [He notes that primitive men are often the quickest to recognize whether missionaries are disinterested or not. If the apostle] does not conduct himself in every respect as a purely spiritual man, but acts also like an agent for his nation, at once his entire ministry becomes suspect to the natives. This would be no better than persuading them that Christianity is the religion of some particular foreign power, and that to embrace Christianity is to submit to the protection and the authority of that power, abandoning one's own nationality. [There is always the same anxiety to safeguard the evident catholicity of the Church. The pope complains of nationalism finding a place in missionary publications during the war.] Ah! This is not the behaviour of the missionary worthy of his name of Catholic missionary. On the contrary, he will never cease to reflect that, being in no sense the missionary of his country but the missionary of Christ, he must so behave that whoever meets him will have no hesitation in recognizing him as the minister of a religion that is not foreign in any nation because she includes all men who worship God in spirit and in truth, and because in her "there is no more Gentile and Jew, no more circumcised and uncircumcised; no one is a barbarian, or Scythian, no one is slave or free man; there is nothing but Christ in any of us" (Col. 3. 11).

Besides this, the missionary will show his love for the country in which he labours by carefully learning the local language; and the pope recalls the recent institution of a centre of specialized studies for Eastern questions, particularly for the learning of languages. The fact must be demonstrated that the Church is the home of all peoples and all languages.

The third part of the Apostolic Letter concerns the duties of Christian countries, which must be earnest in prayer, in producing vocations and alms for the extension of the Kingdom of God. The pope thus reminds Christians of their mission as Catholics, "universal" men. "At this moment," he concludes, "our fatherly love burns to draw into our arms all men alive in the world today. For the Church is always sustained and fortified by the Spirit of God, and it is impossible that the efforts of so many apostles to propagate her should be without result. Their example must raise up a great number of new missionaries who will be sustained by the prayers and the alms of the faithful, and the joy of Christ will be great at the sight of an abundant harvest."

Thus the pope calls on Christendom for a peaceful mobilization for the salvation of souls, and to show forth to greater advantage the catholicity of the Church of God.

The features that make this catholicity shine ever more brilliantly are the implanting of Christianity everywhere and the rise of a native priesthood. We have kept until the end the most beautiful and most significant passage of this Apostolic Letter:

> One final point remains on which the heads of missions are bound particularly to fix their attention: the recruitment and the formation of a native clergy. This is the greatest hope of newly-founded churches, for the native priest is wonderfully prepared to introduce the faith to his compatriots, as is only natural for a man united to them by birth, mentality, sentiments and tastes. Better than any other, he knows what means to use to persuade them, and so frequently he can gain ready access where a foreign priest would not be given permission to enter. It is essential, therefore, that the native clergy be suitably trained and educated if one wants to produce the fruits

for which one hopes. . . . [Their formation] will not simply aim at providing foreign missionaries with helpers just good enough for the humblest duties. The native priest should be made capable of himself governing his compatriots if God should one day call him to be their spiritual leader. For the Church is Catholic; she is not a stranger or a foreigner to any nation or people. It is right, then, that she should draw from each nation such ministers of the Lord as are required for the instruction of their compatriots in true doctrine and for their guidance into the way of salvation. Wherever a native clergy is sufficiently numerous, of sound formation and worthy of their vocation, it may truly be said that in such a place missionary work has achieved its end because a local Church has been successfully founded there. Though persecution should one day raise its ugly head to destroy it, we need not fear that its onslaughts will succeed in shaking its foundations or tearing it up by the roots.

The pope is uncompromising: in this connection there is lost time to be made up, grave omissions to be remedied:

There are regions where Catholicism has been established for several centuries, and where the native clergy to be found are held in low esteem. There exist also peoples who were brought early to the light of the Gospel, who have risen from barbarism and become civilized and produced men second to none in the realms of art and science, and yet, in spite of the beneficial action of the Gospel and the Church during several centuries, have not succeeded in producing bishops to govern them or priests whose prestige could influence their fellow-citizens. It must be recognized, therefore, that so far there has been something wanting or faulty in the education given to priests preparing for missionary life.

In other words, the full meaning of the catholicity of the Church needs to be restored and preserved among missionaries as among Christians of every continent. This letter gave the signal to go forward and since then missionary Christianity lives by that impulse and has even amplified, sustained and organized it. Benedict XV and Cardinal van Rossum were indeed great servants of the Church's catholicity.

Pius XI and the salvation of the world

Since another volume of the present series is devoted to the progress of modern missionary work, we need not treat of it any further. But we should like to show what have been the developments of the idea of catholicity and its sundry manifestations under Pius XI and Pius XII. During the pontificate of Pius XI as also during that of Pius XII, these manifestations have indeed gone far beyond the missionary field. To the latter, therefore, we shall only make brief allusions.

"The peace of Christ in the kingdom of Christ": this formula sums up the two fundamental ideas that inspired the pontificate of Pius XI, and both bear relation to the catholicity of the Church: to establish peace in souls, in families, in society and between nations, and to promote the kingdom of God in the world by means of Catholic Action and the missions. The Encyclical *Ubi arcano Dei* of December 23rd, 1922, sets forth this programme. It recognizes in the modern world the absence of international, social, political, domestic, individual and religious peace. The Church alone can arrest the covetousness and excesses of nationalism.

> There exists a divine institution which alone can safeguard the sacred character of the rights of man, an institution that affects all nations and which is above all nations, invested with sovereign authority and the religious prestige of a magisterium that is supreme and perfect. It is the Church of Christ. She alone is equal to so great a task through the mandate that she holds from God, as also through her very nature and constitution, not forgetting too her incomparable and age-old majesty which the storms of war, far from diminishing, have only succeeded in strengthening in a mysterious manner.

Pius XI then recalls the universal reign of Christ, which was to be the object of a new Encyclical three years later.

On December 11th, 1925, the Encyclical *Quas primas* appeared, which instituted the feast of Christ the King. Now the universal royalty of Christ is one of the foundations of the catholicity of the Church and so is of interest to us here. In the opening pages of this document, the pope speaks of the Missionary Exhibition that had just taken place during the Holy Year, and which had helped Christians to be more mindful of their Catholicism.

> Look first of all at the Missionary Exhibition which made so deep an impression on the minds and hearts of men. There could be seen the endless labours accomplished by the Church to spread the kingdom of her heavenly Bridegroom day by day and more and more over continents and even to islands lost in the midst of the ocean. There could be seen the numerous countries which valiant and invincible missionaries had brought to Catholicism at the cost of their sweat and their blood. There also could be seen the vast territories still to be brought under the sweet and saving domination of our King.

The reality and extension of this universal royalty are established by Pius XI by appeal to the Scriptures and Christian tradition. Christ reigns over men by natural right and by acquired right: "From this doctrine, common to all the books of holy Scripture, this consequence naturally follows: Since she is the kingdom of Christ on earth, called to include all men and countries of the universe, the Catholic Church must hail, in her Author and Founder, the Sovereign Lord, the King of kings, by multiple signs of veneration in the course of the annual cycle of the liturgy."

In this same document Pius XI transcribes a passage from Leo XIII's *Annum sacrum* (1899): "Christ's empire does not extend exclusively to Catholic countries, nor only to baptized Christians who juridically belong to the Church, even if they have been led far from her by erroneous opinions, or separated from her communion by schism. It embraces equally and without exception all men, even those who know nothing of the Christian faith, so that the empire of Jesus Christ is in strict truth the universality of the human race."

The annual feast of Christ the King reminds Christians of the urgent need there is of working for the extension of the kingdom of God in the world, so that the fact corresponds to the principle. The apostolic ambitions of the Church are thus founded on a doctrine that is as solid as it is stimulating, as exciting as it is pressing.

The same preoccupation to stimulate the prayers and expiations of Christians for the establishment of the peace of Christ is found again in the Encyclical *Caritate Christi compulsi* (May 3rd, 1932). Here, recognizing the terrible consequences of the economic crisis in which all men were struggling, Pius XI wishes to put an end to these hatreds, injustices and divisions, by instigating a campaign of prayer and penitence in honour of the Sacred Heart of Jesus. Pius XI condemns exaggerated nationalism and hatred between peoples, he reminds Christians of their universal mission and their worldwide responsibility, he is anxious that they should deserve their beautiful name of Catholics.

Meanwhile he had spoken and worked for the extension of God's kingdom in the whole world. Beginning in 1923, he had created in the Latin Church a native episcopate, successively conferred upon Indians, Chinese, Japanese and Annamites. . . . The great Encyclical *Rerum Ecclesiae* (1926) took up again with even greater precision the themes and directives of Benedict XV. On other occasions also he sought to put missionaries on their guard against the spirit of nationalism. Thus in December 1929: "In no way whatsoever must the missions spread the spirit of nationalism, but solely Catholicism, the true apostolate. They must be at the service of souls, and only souls. Nationalism has always been a scourge and a curse for the missions; it is no exaggeration to say so. For all missionaries, one may say for all those called to labour in the apostolate in any way, from the humblest priest to the pope himself, nationalism, for all the advantages that it appears sometimes to have brought with it, has brought nothing but trouble."

Just as his predecessors had gradually freed the missions from Spanish and Portuguese patronage so was he instrumental in totally extricating them from French protection which extended to the missions of the Near East and to those of China in the course of the nineteenth century. In 1922, an Apostolic Delegate was installed in China and a full council took place at Shanghai in 1924. A similar delegation was established in Indo-China the following year. A letter addressed in 1926 to the Vicars Apostolic in China protested against the accusation of national particularism: "The truth is that the very name by which the Church is known— Catholic—proves that she extends to all nations and embraces all peoples, and that the divine will of Christ her Founder forbids her to make any interior distinction between races and social classes."

The pure manifestation of the Church's independence and catholicity was so dear to Pius XI that several of his most solemn and striking acts had as their object and intention the preservation of the Church from all particularism: the racial particularism of the Nazis, the nationalistic particularism of the Fascists, the ideological particularism of Communism. Two Encyclicals appeared on the same day, March 14th, 1937; *Mit brennender Sorge* against German National Socialism, and *Divini Redemptoris* against atheistic Communism. The first condemned the cult of a nation, or a race, and strongly affirmed the catholicity of the Bride, the continuation of Christ, in opposition to pagan doctrines:

> The Church founded by the Redeemer is one, the same for all peoples and nations. Under her mighty dome which, like the firmament, covers the whole earth, is a home-country for all peoples and all languages, there is a place for the development of all individual qualities, all special advantages, every kind of work and vocation given by God the Creator and Saviour as much to individuals as to whole races. The motherly heart of the Church is great enough and wide enough to recognize, in the perfecting of these characters and personal gifts that God has willed, rather the wealth of variety than the danger of divergence.

The second Encyclical repudiates, among other things, hatred that is the antithesis of the universalism of love, and seeks to show how Christianity is above all parties and extremes that cause divisions: "This (Christian) doctrine remains equally far from the errors of all extremes, as also from the exaggerations of parties and the systems attached to them; she ever keeps the balance of justice and truth; she demands the just measure in theory and assures its progressive realization in practice, taking care to reconcile the rights and duties of all, etc."

By her transcendence and her catholicity, Christianity shows her independence and repudiation of all partisan exclusivism; she would be equally mutilated by Communism, which makes use of class hatred as a factor for political domination, as by anti-semite, war-loving Nazism that makes an idol of race.

Even before he started to combat these forms of particularism and to condemn them in the name of the one and only God, Pius XI had already withstood the encroachments and narrow nationalism of Mussolini's Fascist movement. In 1931, an Encyclical, *Non abbiamo bisogno*, was launched against the claims of the Duce's government. It dealt chiefly with the question of Catholic Action and the education of youth, but the matters at stake in the battle that was to continue until the death of Pius XI can be seen in an informal address given to the students of the College of Propaganda in 1938, of which a report in the third person, as was Pius XI's preference, has been preserved:

> The Pope has just received a new communication [about Racism]. He is always grateful to those who provide him with information, even if what they have to say is anything but agreeable. On the contrary, he is even more grateful when the news received is painful, because it is an indication that there is something to be done in that direction. . . . Catholic means universal, not racist, or nationalist, in the dividing sense of these two attributes. . . . Catholic action must draw its

inspiration from these principles. This is indispensable, because Catholic Action means Catholic life, and it is for this very reason that Catholic Action is like the apple of the Pope's eye. . . . Catholic Action is in the Church, in the Catholic Church. The Pope goes so far as to say that it *is* the Church, because Catholic Action is Catholic life. Catholic Action, like the Catholic Church, is Catholic. Its intention is to be Catholic, that is, universal; the word Catholic has no other meaning. . . . Human beings are one single race, universal, "catholic". Nevertheless there is no denying that within this universal race there is room for special races and endless variety, as also for many nationalities even more specialized. And as in a great musical composition we hear some general theme which pervades a multitude of variations of different tonalities, intonations and expressions, so among human beings there exists one great human race that is universal, "catholic", one great and universal human family, and within it much variety. . . .

This is typical of Pius XI's style: an eloquence that is, so to speak, hammered out, where the idea jostles the words, repeats them, seems to tangle them up and yet the predominant thought is fully apparent in all its strength, surging forth from the indomitable will of a pope who was never known to cringe before the mighty ones of this world. The word *catholic* is repeated like a war cry, a leitmotiv, a predominant idea from which nothing will turn him aside.

The same thought had been expressed with much feeling at the International Congress of Catholic Youth in 1925:

You are here as representatives of the Catholic Youth International. Well, my dear sons, think a little of another International, of which you are no more than a fraction, although a magnificent fraction: the Church, that holy, venerable, incomparable mother of souls, of men, of the centuries. In her we see the true International which, in very truth, covers the whole world, for even where civilization ends, where neither arts nor commerce nor industry nor science have yet penetrated, there our great and holy Mother has entered by faith and charity. And our Missionary Exhibition, which you have certainly visited or intend to visit (it is well worth it, even after visiting the wonderful basilicas and catacombs), this Exhibition tells you how this divine International which is the Catholic Church reaches out to the furthest frontiers. And you have come here to see her at her very centre, and to embrace her, as it were, in her entirety with a single look and to taste of her beauty, while you yourselves, by your presence here, add yet more to this vision of greatness and power. See her then, the great, the divine International, the one you sing about, the one you acknowledge in the Creed: *Credo unam, sanctam, catholicam, apostolicam Ecclesiam.* There she is, standing before you, one and universal! The unity and the universality of the Church! They have never been more clearly visible, they show themselves in daily events during this Holy Year, and with what brilliance! As for the universality, it is you yourselves who contribute your share to show forth its wonder.

Pius XI's successor was to speak of the supra-nationality of the Church, he himself spoke more of it as the great International. It is the same thought under two different aspects. Pius XI frequently extolled, in his discourses, that spirit expressed by the untranslatable Italian *Romanità*—devotion to and pride in Rome—but only as the centre of a Church that is universal, the centre of universal activity. He was quick to grasp the importance of the radio both as a symbol of this universal activity and also as a means for use in its service. On February 12th, 1931, in the presence of Marconi, he inaugurated the Vatican Radio Station, and began his message in these lyrical terms:

To the whole world! Having been chosen by the secret design of God's providence as successor to the Prince of the Apostles, whose doctrine and preaching are destined by God's command to reach every creature, and being the first Pontiff to be able to make use of the admirable invention of Marconi, we use this occasion to speak to all men and things in the words of holy Scripture, now and always, "Listen, O heavens, to what I have to say, and let the earth attend to the words of my mouth. Harken, ye nations; hear, all ye who dwell in the earth, being one human people, rich and poor united in the same thought; Listen, ye continents and distant peoples. . . ."

The pope called upon God first and then addressed all Catholics, the hierarchy, religious, missionaries, all the faithful, non-Catholic dissidents, rulers, workmen and employers, the sick and suffering, finishing by giving the Apostolic Blessing *Urbi et orbi*. This important discourse forms a beautiful charter for the radio and ought to be better known.

This same famous message is also a moving symbol of the catholicity of the Church of today and of its determination to "baptize" and Christianize not only the greatest human discoveries, but the whole of humanity and the cosmos.

From the brief and partial quotations made, we can conclude that the pontificate of Pius XI was illustrious by a magnificent unfolding of the Church's catholicity. In an enslaved and divided world, eaten up with hatred, the Church has shown her face of universalism and love.

Pius XII's teaching

A few months after Pius XII had been raised to the pontifical throne, the second world war broke out, bringing darkness and bloodshed to the first six years of his pontificate. From such times of severe trial our faith should come forth purified, revived, dedicated once again to a more beautiful future, whatever trials beset the life of Christians and humanity in general. The first world war was followed by an increased refulgence of the Church's catholicity which shines even more brilliantly after the second, in spite of a world in which peaceful coexistence is often no more than a word, where parties confront each other and particularism of all kinds divides and oppresses the human race. Here again we shall make only brief allusions to the missionary work of Pius XII, concentrating rather in a broader and more complete manner on his labours for the catholicity of the Church. In this connection we must consider successively his doctrine and his acts.

The new pope's first Encyclical, *Summi Pontificatus* (October 1939), immediately proclaimed this supra-nationality of the Church and sketched the major preoccupations of the pontificate. The Encyclical is particularly opposed to the deification of the State, a form of particularism that was much in evidence and especially harmful at that time, but he recalls the Church's respect for particular characteristics in each nation and draws attention above all to the unity of the human race: "First among the pernicious errors so widespread today is the deliberate forgetting of the law of human solidarity and charity, dictated and imposed as much by community of origin and the equality of rational nature among all men of whatever race, as by the redeeming sacrifice offered by Jesus Christ on the altar of the Cross to his heavenly Father on behalf of sinful humanity."

Pius XII goes on to specify the forms in which this unity is found: unity of nature, unity of the immediate end of man and his mission in the world, unity of supernatural end, unity of means to attain that end.

This masterly Encyclical, however, was only the beginning, the preamble of doctrinal teaching that was to increase steadily with the years. The summit is reached, no doubt, in Pius XII's Christmas message of 1945 and the discourse made to the new Cardinals in February 1946. In the Christmas message he said:

The Catholic Church, of which Rome is the centre, is supra-national by its very essence. This is to be understood in two senses: one negative, the other positive. The Church is a mother, *sancta Mater Ecclesia*, a real mother, the mother of all nations and all peoples as well as of each individual. And precisely because she is a mother, she neither belongs nor can belong exclusively to one people more than to another, but to all equally. She is a mother, and consequently she is not nor can be a stranger or foreigner in any place; she lives, or should live by reason of her very nature, among all peoples. Moreover, as a mother with her husband and children form one family, so the Church, in virtue of an incomparably closer union, constitutes, what is greater and better than a family, the mystical Body of Christ. Thus the Church is supranational, since she makes up one indivisible and universal whole.

Pius XII's discourse on February 20th, 1946, states this doctrine more precisely by replying to an objection or a possible error:

We must take care, however, not to think of the Church after the manner of an earthly empire that wishes to embrace the whole of human society. The conception of the Church as an earthly empire with worldly domination is utterly false. . . . In accomplishing the mandate of her divine Founder to spread into the entire world and conquer every creature for the Gospel (Mark 16. 15), the Church is not an empire, especially in the imperialistic sense generally associated with the word empire today. Her progress and her expansion lead her by a way that is the very reverse of modern imperialism. Her progress is primarily one of depth, and only then in scope and extension. Her first concern is to discover man himself, and to form him, to model him, to perfect in him the likeness to God. Her work is accomplished in the depths of each man's heart, but its repercussions are felt all through life, in every field of individual action. . . . If, at certain times in history and in certain places, some particular civilization or some special nation or social class has made its influence on the Church felt more than others, this does not mean that she was subjected to any one of them, nor that at some particular time in history she was, so to speak, turned to stone and closed to all further development. On the contrary, bending over man with an ever attentive ear, listening to every beat of his heart, she knows his every aspiration with that clear-sighted intuition and that penetrating ingenuity which can only spring from the supernatural light of Christ's doctrine and the supernatural warmth of divine charity. And so the Church follows her way without hesitation or collision along the providential road of times and circumstances. Such is the deep meaning of her vital law of continual adaptation. Some of her enemies, incapable of appreciating so lofty a conception, have sometimes interpreted this as opportunism. No, the universal comprehension of the Church has nothing suggestive of the narrowness of a sect nor of the exclusiveness of an imperialism that is a prisoner to its own tradition.

It is unfortunate that we can only quote in part so masterly a text of such great consequence. The Christmas message of 1945 must at all costs be quoted again, containing as it does a passage that, in our opinion, expresses most clearly the progress both of the idea of catholicity and of its concrete realization in modern times. Once Catholics of Europe and America have really grasped what it is that Pius XII says here, the cause of practical catholicity will be won.

In former times the visible life of the Church showed forth her strength by preference in the countries of ancient Europe, from which she flowed, like a majestic river, to the ends of the world. Today, on the contrary, she reveals a constant exchange of life and energy between all the members of the mystical Body of Christ on earth. In other continents there are many countries that have long since outstripped the missionary stage of their ecclesiastical organization and are governed by their own hierarchy, contributing to the whole Church both material and spiritual benefits of which, formerly, they were only the recipients. As Christ took a real human nature, so the Church also takes on herself the fullness of all that is authentically human and makes of it a channel of supernatural life. . . . She lives and develops in all the countries of the world, and all these countries contribute to her life and development.

Thus, according to Pope Pius XII, the Church is the scene of universal exchanges; in her and by her the fullness of Christ and the fullness of mankind are united.

On other occasions, Pius XII has drawn the inferences from these principles. We mention two of them here: the Church is not bound to any particular civilization or culture; she has every respect and encouragement for the diversity of civilizations and cultures.

As regards the first, the teaching of Pius XII is so complete and so frequently repeated that we can only quote one example chosen from among many.

Speaking to the Congress of Historical Sciences on September 7th, 1955, he said:

> The Church is aware that she has received her mission and her task for all times to come and for all men, and consequently she is in no way bound to any single determined culture. . . . The Catholic Church does not identify herself with any culture; her essence makes such a thing impossible. Nevertheless, she is ready to treat with all cultures. She recognizes and sanctions anything in them that is not contrary to nature. But into each of them she introduces also the truth and grace of Jesus Christ, and so confers on them His likeness. By this means, she contributes most effectively towards the peace of the world.

As regards respect for local cultures and customs, Pius XII on several occasions spoke his mind with all the clarity that could be wished. In his great missionary Encyclical he said:

> One point remains that we would wish to see perfectly grasped by all. Since her origin down to our own days, the Church has always followed that most wise norm according to which the Gospel does not destroy or extinguish anything that is good, upright and beautiful in the character and genius of those that embrace it. Indeed, when the Church exhorts races to rise up under the guidance of the Christian religion to a higher level of humanity and culture, she does not act like the man who, respecting nothing, cuts down a luxuriant forest, causing havoc and ruin on all sides, but rather like the gardener who grafts valuable cuttings on to wild stock so that it may one day produce sweeter and more palatable fruit. In spite of the stain inherited from the sad fall of Adam, human nature retains a substratum that is naturally Christian which, clarified by divine light and nourished by grace, can be raised to real virtue and to supernatural life. This is why the Church has never treated pagan doctrines with disdain and contempt, but has rather sought to free them from what is erroneous in them and then to perfect them by crowning

them with Christian wisdom. Similarly, with their art and culture, which has sometimes reached a very high standard, she welcomes it kindly, cultivates it with care and brings it to a degree of beauty to which it had never before attained. Neither has she condemned outright, but rather sought to sanctify, the manners and customs of particular peoples, together with their traditional institutions (*Evangelii praecones*).

We see then that the Church's catholicity obliges her to welcome everything that is good, to incorporate it within herself, to Christianize it for God's glory and the good of mankind.

Pius XII's work

One of the first acts of the new pope in 1939 was to extend to China the benefit of certain liberal decisions made in the time of Pius XI to resolve certain "questions of rites" for the benefit of Manchuria and Japan. This was not a matter of the liturgy in Chinese or Japanese, but of certain gestures of respect towards Confucius and ancestors, remote and recent. These gestures had been proscribed in the eighteenth century because of their religious and superstitious connection, but were allowed to Christians of the twentieth century because, on the admission of the civil authorities, they no longer had anything more than a purely civil and civic significance. In this way one of the most formidable obstacles to the conversion of Asians ceased to exist; Christians could take their full share in national life, and their religion became a religion of their own locality, taking root there without losing its universal character.

To emphasize still further this indigenous character of Christianity in all parts of the world, Pius XII solemnly set up the regular episcopal hierarchy in many countries. Without ceasing to be attached to the Congregation *de Propaganda Fide*, local Churches would henceforth be under the guidance and authority, no longer of vicars apostolic acting as lieutenants of the pope, but of real archbishops and bishops, as in the older parts of Christendom. These young Churches thus reached maturity. This was the case for South Africa, China, most of the English colonies in Africa, and, in November 1955, the French colonies of Africa. This step finds its explanation, as also its inspiration, in the doctrine of the supranationality of the Church rather than in giving satisfaction to national pride.

At the same time, official relations were established between the Vatican and various Christian nations. Even while the war was still in progress, Japan (1942) and then China (1943) sent an accredited representative to the Holy See. In 1947, China sent to Rome as her plenipotentiary the celebrated convert Dr J. Wu, well known by reason of his spiritual autobiography *Beyond East and West*. This great man of letters, after assimilating the various religious conceptions of his people and for a short time giving his adherence to Protestantism, is himself a good example of catholicity and the presage of a China that is both traditional and Christian.

Countries that had recently won their independence hastened in turn to send their representatives to the Vatican: Lebanon, Mohammedan countries like Egypt and Syria, India, Indonesia, Vietnam, etc. On each occasion Pope Pius XII took the opportunity either of praising a worthy Christian past, faithful and sturdy as a cedar, or else appreciating the spiritual value of ancient civilizations. These were occasions, therefore, of showing the breadth of the Church's vision and her universal interests. Close bonds were formed which, besides forwarding the cause of peace, also helped the development of the faith and the union of all the faithful in a common front against atheistic materialism. A representative of the Holy See was sent in return to each of these countries. Never before was the Vatican in diplomatic relations with so many countries containing non-Christian majorities. The pope's relations with the world at large were thus made easier, and scarcely a month went by without his receiving Jewish, Mohammedan or Buddhist delegations.

Until 1946, Italian Cardinals formed a considerable majority in the Sacred College. But from then on, at the express wish of Pius XII and to express better the Church's universality, the proportion was reversed, so that now foreign Cardinals hold a considerable majority over the Italians. Of the thirty-two Cardinals nominated in 1946, one was Chinese, one an Armenian Patriarch, one a Portuguese, the Archbishop of Lourenço-Marquès in Mozambique, to represent Africa. A few years later, the Indian Archbishop of Bombay, Cardinal Gracias, came to take his place in the Church's Senate.

In his Christmas message of 1945, Pius XII gave the reasons for his decision:

> It is our wish that by these nominations a greater number of races and peoples within the Catholic community should be represented in such a way as to assure the principle of the Church's universality. And just as we welcomed into the Vatican, as a result of the war, men from all over the world, so now that the war is over, we have the consolation of seeing around us men from every corner of the world taking their place in our Sacred College. For the Vatican City is the universal City on which are fixed the eyes of catholicity.

He could not have said more clearly how anxious he was that the government of the Church should be more international, so as to be a more perfect image of the universality of Christ's Mystical Body. No doubt this will continue to be a preoccupation of the Popes.

The stability and growth of the Church in the various countries of the world is conditioned by the growth of local clergy and laity. The number of native priests and bishops greatly increased from the beginning of Pius XII's pontificate. A very significant gesture illustrates his anxious care in this respect. On October 29, 1939, just after the second world war had embarked upon its career of death, in the face of racial fanaticism fighting for world domination, Pius XII determined to consecrate twelve bishops with his own hands in Rome. Side by side at this new Pentecost were representatives of nations at war, the first black-skinned and also the first Madagascan bishop. It was the feast of Christ the King, when the Preface of the Mass proclaims the universal reign of justice, love and peace of the Son of God. In one of his first solemn gestures, Pius XII struck a direct blow at colour prejudice, affirming the equality of races in God's sight and the Church's identical love for her children of all nations.

Since that date, nominations of native bishops have steadily increased. In 1940, every diocese in Japan was under the rule of native bishops or administrators. In Africa and Asia there is a rapid increase in the number of bishops chosen from the local clergy; in January 1956 there were no less than 125 such. In 1955 alone, fifteen native bishops of the Latin rite were consecrated. The object aimed at, according to the words of Pius XII, is "that the Church may be firmly and permanently established in new countries and may receive its own hierarchy, chosen from among the inhabitants of the place".

The allocution to the new Cardinals in 1946 strongly emphasized the importance of the laity in the Church. Pius XII said: "They above all must be increasingly aware not only that they belong to the Church, but of being themselves the Church. . . . They are the Church."

In accordance with this principle and with the intention of planting the Church ever more firmly all over the world, Pius XII constantly encouraged the training and action of the Christian laity everywhere.

The lay missionary is already working for this end, and it is noteworthy that Pius XII was the first to mention him and express his delight at this development in an official document (the Encyclical of 1951). But his chief care was for the ordinary layman in all countries. Hence his pressing invitation, in the same document, to form new groups of Catholic Action; hence also the world-wide organization of the apostolate of the laity.

After a first general Congress dealing with this subject in Rome in 1951, two regional Congresses took place, one for Africa at Kisubi (Uganda) at the end of 1953; the other for South-East Asia as Manila (Philippines) at the end of 1955. The first was successful in showing African laity how serious this matter is for them and how grave their responsibility. The other, coming as it did after successful local congresses, particularly in India, had the advantage of bringing together again the lay directors of South-East Asia. Pius XII never ceased from calling upon Christian laymen to throw themselves with all their faith into the various departments of Catholic Action in universities, trade unions and in the social, civil and political spheres. It depends on them to see that the rapid evolution of many countries in the world is accomplished in an atmosphere of collaboration and mutual respect.

At Pius XII's request, the conference of Catholic International Organizations made contact with missionaries and the Christian laity in the effort to relieve the misery of undernourished and under-developed regions. In the international sphere, moreover, the eminent place occupied by Pius XII and the efforts he made to restore or maintain peace, are well known. His Christmas messages of 1954 and 1955 both insisted on the need for conversations between mother-countries and states dependent on them to help on the cause of their autonomy with a regard for personal rights and the preservation of mutual ties. The Church ever claims to be the mother of all people, builder of peace and universal brotherhood. Bishops in many lands have borne witness to this superior and Catholic view of things.

Yet another sphere of action in which Pius XII revealed his anxiety to assert the Church's catholicity is that of liturgical adaptation. An authoritative and informed writer, Mgr Paventi, tells us:

As regards liturgical language, permission was granted in 1941 and 1942 to the missions in New Guinea, China and Japan, Indo-China, India and Africa, to translate and use the

Rituale in native languages. In the prayers, anointings, exorcisms and sacramentals, the Latin language is to be used only for what concerns the essence of the rite. Similar permission was also granted to Indonesia. In 1949 the use of high Chinese was allowed within the limits of China itself, even for the Mass, except for the Canon which must be in Latin (*La Chiesa missionaria*, Rome, 1949).

To these permissions we may add that given (quite readily it seems) to several African territories to *sing* the first part of the Mass in native languages, and also to develop their own style of sacred art of which Cardinal Costantini was a pioneer; he exhibited some masterpieces of native art in Rome in the Holy Year (1950), and subsequently in Madrid and Lisbon. The Encyclical *Musicae sacrae* (December 25th, 1955) encouraged the use of hymns with both words and music of native origin, although it continues to give pride of place to Gregorian chant, the symbol and expression of the Church's unity. In this Encyclical Pius XII said:

> The messengers of the Gospel in pagan lands must be ready, while carrying out their apostolic work, to develop this love for religious music, already so strong in those they hope to convert. The religious hymns of these peoples are frequently admired, even by civilized peoples. Missionaries should therefore provide Christian hymns, in a similar idiom, to counteract the pagan ones. These new hymns will celebrate in song the truths of our faith, the life of Christ our Lord, and the praises of the Blessed Virgin Mary and the saints, but in a language and music familiar to those peoples.

Thus we constantly meet applications of the fundamental principle of the catholicity and the supra-nationality of the Church. She is the mother of all peoples and all peoples should feel at their ease in this universal Church.

To realize how greatly Pius XII had at heart this care for the Church's catholicity, we have only to recall his many addresses to people of every nationality, of various religions, different social classes and professions, and see how he responded to the manifold aspirations of the man of today. We have only to notice how he beatified and canonized Christians of various countries and all social conditions, how he intervened in questions concerning peace among nations and mutual universal understanding in the multiple international problems of the hour. But since the pope is not himself the whole Church, we must add a word about the various expressions of catholicity furnished by present-day Christianity.

Taking first the intellectual order, mention must be made of all those whose intellectual activity is both a manifestation and an enrichment of the Church's catholicity, although a complete catalogue of this would outstep the limits of this work. In this class we must include not only historians and theologians of the mission, but also theologians of the Church (such as Fathers de Lubac, Congar, Monsignor Journet, etc.); ethnologists such as Aupiais, Schmidt, van Bulck; all those who share in the work of evangelization of the Church and the glorifying of God by discoveries, of bringing the faith into the various departments of human activity: explorers, scholars, technicians of modern means of expression, etc. All these, in various ways, bear witness to the universal vocation of the Church and to her capacity for embracing human and cosmic reality in its entirety.

But the Church of today is not content simply to think about these things and busy herself with research work. Above all, she lives, and this present life of the Church is without doubt the clearest proof and the most eloquent manifestation of her catholicity, because she ever makes real this historical moral miracle: unity in diversity, within a universal body whose limits coincide with those of the earth, and which maintains its youth and vigour after two thousand years. The Church, rich in the most divers and least similar forms of holiness, rich in piety that varies infinitely in its expression yet all springs from the same source, rich in acts of faith, hope and charity that vary with each continent, each nation or social class, even with each individual. One has only to think of the way in which an African, a Chinaman, an Indian, an Irishman, a Spaniard, an American understand and live their Christian life. Or again, a child, an intellectual, a peasant, a student, Catholic prayer has many aspects, the apostolate many forms, theology its particular emphasis and approach in each country, art its variety from nation to nation, even the dress and manner of the clergy differs from country to country. Social works, charitable works, Catholic Action are revealed in a multitude of ways. Nevertheless it is the same Church everywhere, the same *Credo*, the same submission to the Roman Pontiff. Truly does twentieth-century Christianity offer the sociologist strange motives for wonder and admiration, an infinite field for observation and analysis.

Here and there indeed one finds an undercurrent of narrow-mindedness and the spirit of particularism that would soon tend, if not checked by the hierarchy, to reduce the Church to a sect, a "ghetto". But these influences are opposed, condemned, denied by the greater part of Christendom. Certain archaic and over-rigid conceptions, such as that of Fr Feeney in the United States about the salvation of non-Catholics, have been roundly condemned and proscribed by the Church. For, while scrupulously and faithfully keeping the deposit of faith, the Church can present it in a manner that will respond to the aspirations of men of every age and every continent. The Church in no way disavows any part of her true tradition, but she will by no means lock herself up in the past. She is conscious and proud of the diversity in the minds and mentality of her members and is careful to preserve all that is of real value in men of every age and country. She will not allow any individual group the monopoly of integral orthodoxy.

In the second chapter of this work we showed how the catholicity of the Church is, at the same time, a given reality or an endowment and also a progressive reality or something that is gradually acquired; the Church has always both to defend it and encourage its growth. Facts constrain us to think that the Church of the twentieth century is in a healthy condition as regards this point. A passage of Fr de Montcheuil's *Aspects de l'Église* may well serve as a conclusion for this chapter and as a plan of action for the future.

Catholicism is not merely a religion; it *is* religion. In it, all religious aspiration given by God to every human being should find its purpose and its end. This aspiration has one identical substance for all men, since it comes from God and returns to the same God, but it is expressed by natures that have each their originality. The Church guides along the one path all the authentic spiritual resources that she finds in each. Thus she alone is able to bring to light all the wealth she has within her. When great civilizations, like those of India and China for example, have been thoroughly penetrated by the Church, new forms of religious life will appear, genuinely Catholic, that is, truly inspired by the Church, expressing the same faith in the same unity, but different from those with which we are familiar. Certain Christian values that we are perhaps slow to appreciate will then come into evidence. And the whole Christian world will benefit by this. For . . . the Church is not content merely to save and develop each individual in his particular line, but establishes between all a current of communion, so that the treasures of each may be of profit to all. Catholicity does not consist solely in the ability and the wish to reach all men and all peoples, but in the ability and the wish to gather them all together into one, not imposing a rigid uniformity on them, but maintaining their differences. Outside her unity, these latter frequently cause exasperation in misunderstandings and hostility; within her, they harmonize and perfect each other.

And further on the same author adds: "Because she (the Church) is Catholic, she is opposed to all that separates and is exclusive, but she also is opposed to spiritual uniformity for the same reason."

CONCLUSION:

THE CATHOLIC SPIRIT

Immediately after the passage quoted at the end of the last chapter, Fr de Montcheuil makes the following observation about the Church:

It is important that the Church's children should not provoke misunderstandings about her attitude in those around her. *Catholicity should live in every Christian.* A true Catholic is not merely a person who belongs to the Catholic Church. To be worthy of the name Catholic, one must first learn to appreciate the differences of others, to understand them and to love them as such. This is to repudiate the sectarian spirit, which gives absolute and universal value to forms of particularism. To appreciate what in others appears to be trivial and disuniting, the true Catholic will consult the Church, not his own personal preferences. He dreads nothing so much as to close the door or to make access to the Church more difficult for some soul by giving the impression, by word or action, that such a soul must renounce things to which he is legitimately attached. More than this, when the occasion arises the true Catholic will sincerely try to profit by the differences of others; he does not suppose that he is already in possession of everything, he does not shut himself up within his own mind; he is not eager to copy all that he sees of thought and action in others, but he is quick to observe anything there that can be assimilated by him. The true Catholic must ever keep himself within this current of vital exchange that passes through the Church, and draw all he can from it, wishing that it may extend to the very limits of humanity. To see in the Church nothing but a beautiful external organization is, as we have said, to understand nothing about it. But it is equally absurd and harmful to see the Church as a sect, something incomplete, which acknowledges its own boundaries and is content to remain within them, when all the time she seeks to penetrate all, to unite all and enliven all in fruitful exchange.

These grave words, so deep and practical, express the essential of what we wish to say in these last pages. They should be thought over carefully, but even more should be put into practice. We shall only suggest certain applications of them. The first is that we should put ourselves in the place of others, to judge them with understanding and the justice that we should claim for our own customs and behaviour, both religious and national. In this connection, we reproduce an instruction of the Congregation for the Propagation of the Faith of June 9th, 1939. It is far too little known and deserves to be quoted in full, for the principle analysed so delicately here is of value in many other connections.

The Sacred Congregation of Propaganda has observed more than once that in official reports or works devoted to the missionary apostolate, as also in sermons and on public occasions, it happens that the manners, religion, national genius and conditions of life of those to whom we should bring the Catholic faith, are described in colours that show up more what is bad in them than what is good. Admittedly, this is done without the least bad intention and doubtless with the sole purpose of stirring up greater love for our brethren still deprived of the light of Christ and of augmenting the resources for the furthering of works of piety and charity. Nevertheless, it cannot be denied that to act in this way is to show a grave lack of that mutual courtesy so necessary between peoples, it is an offence against equity and justice and may justly provoke the indignation of the people spoken of in this way. It is easy to imagine our feelings if foreigners used similar language about our own country.

Such an attitude is to be avoided at all costs, the more so since it may produce a false idea about missionaries, injurious to their persons and fatal to the success of their apostolate. It will be thought that they do not approach non-Christians with that charity of heart which, instead of judging others after their own model, opens the mind generously and sincerely to understand, appreciate and love them.

That is why the Sacred Congregation of Propaganda recommends earnestly all those who have to treat of missionary matters, by writing or speech, to speak of other nations with the same delicacy that they would hope to hear in the mouths of foreigners speaking of their own country. To succeed in this, they must never lose sight of the fact that, among the nations open to the missionary apostolate, many are worthy of the greatest respect by reason of the antiquity and nobility of their culture and civilization. Naturally, then, they are embittered and resent strongly being treated as though there were no difference between them and those races generally admitted to be less advanced, to use the current expression. Finally, it is not permissible to exaggerate certain particular cases so as to bring on a whole people a judgement both injurious and false. In this connection St Paul has left us an injunction which it is our duty to follow with constant and faithful attention: We are careful not to give offence to anybody, lest we should bring discredit on our ministry; as God's ministers, we must do everything to make ourselves acceptable (2 Cor. 6. 3–4).

The precision and psychological delicacy of this text renders any long commentary unnecessary. It speaks of justice, understanding, love of non-Christian people and their countries. But who can fail to see that its lesson goes far beyond the object for which it was written? As its title declares, it is not simply a matter "of the manner in which missionary questions are to be treated and the prudence they demand", nor even of the general attitude of the individual missionary, but rather of the behaviour of every Catholic towards collective realities and individual persons in the midst of an unbelieving or non-Christian world. We must love them all as ourselves, treating them and judging them as we ourselves would wish to be treated and judged. We must not only respect the differences we see in others but, provided it is not a matter of sin, love those differences and wish prudently to be enriched by them, ourselves and the whole Christian world.

The second and final application we should like to make of the principles set down by Fr de Montcheuil concerns our attitude towards Catholics of other nations or with a mentality differing from our own. Men of most nations have much to learn in the way of sympathetic understanding shown to people of other cultures and other religions. Catholics of each nation have much to learn from Catholics of other nations, especially from those who have ways of looking at things differing from their own. The Church does not confine herself to one nation, nor to one way of thought or piety. She admits diversity and differences and wishes us not merely to tolerate them but to make the effort to respect, understand and love them and to be the richer for so doing.

St Augustine has lessons for us that are always to the point. He says: "I know not who it is who limits charity to the land of Africa. Stretch forth your charity over the whole world, if you would truly love Christ, because the members of Christ are spread all through the world."

To love our brethren in Christ is to pray for them and to accept them as they are, with all that differentiates them from ourselves. Such differences are an expression of the riches of God and of Christ. To be the universal brother, as Fr de Foucauld wished to be, but primarily to be the universal brother of Catholics all over the world. To support them as members of our own family, to do the impossible to understand them better, and to take in good part their opinions or their manners, as St Ignatius recommends at the beginning of his Exercises. To show greater interest in what they are and what they do, in their difficulties and their problems, above all when they are engulfed in the whirlwind of persecution, like our brethren in China today.

It is greatly to be desired that courses of religious instruction, study circles, the Catholic press and literature should inform us with ever growing sympathy and accuracy about these forms of Catholicism in other nations and the variety of mentality in present-day Catholics. Instead of treating each other with culpable thoughtlessness we should seek rather to know one another better, to esteem one another more, to try to distinguish between what belongs to the political or social order in our positions from what is authentically religious. We have something to learn from all Catholics, we must embrace them all in the same love, we must have for all the solicitude of the Church in their regard, the love of God, the tenderness of Christ.

SELECT BIBLIOGRAPHY

ATTWATER, Donald: *Eastern Catholic Worship*, New York, Devin Adair, 1945.

DE LUBAC, Henri, S.J.: *Catholicism, a study of Dogma in Relation to the Corporate Destiny of Mankind*, translated by Lancelot C. Sheppard, London, Burns Oates, 1950, and New York, Sheed and Ward.

LEBRETON, Jules, S.J.: *Life and Teaching of Jesus Christ our Lord*, London, Burns Oates, and New York, Macmillan.

LEBRETON, Jules, S.J., and ZEILLER, Jacques: *The History of the Primitive Church*, translated by Ernest C. Messenger, four volumes, London, Burns Oates, 1942–8, and New York, Macmillan.

SHEED, F. J.: *Theology and Sanity*, London and New York, Sheed and Ward, 1948.

The papal encyclicals, etc., quoted in the text may be consulted in:

FREMANTLE, Anne: *Papal Encyclicals in their Historical Context*, New York, Putnam, 1956.

Single encyclicals are published in English by The Catholic Truth Society of London as pamphlets: Pius XI, *Divini Redemptoris, Mortalium Animos, Quas Primas*, etc.; Pius XII, *Summi Pontificatus, Mystici Corporis*, etc., and by the N.C.W.C. of Washington, D.C.